130 Mini Quilt Blocks

A Collection of Exquisite Patchwork Blocks
Using Ready-made Fabric Bundles

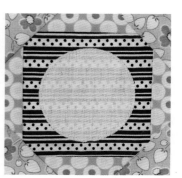

130 Mini Quilt Blocks

A Collection of Exquisite Patchwork Blocks Using Ready-made Fabric Bundles

Susan Briscoe

St. Martin's Griffin
New York

Contents

Library of Congress Cataloging-in-
Publication Data available upon request.

ISBN: 978-0-312-67530-1

QUAR.SMAB

Conceived, designed, and produced by
Quarto Publishing plc
The Old Brewery
6 Blundell Street
London N7 9BH

Project Editor: Diana Craig
Art Editor: Jackie Palmer
Editor: Sally MacEachern
Designer: Simon Brewster
Photographer: Simon Pask
Art Director: Caroline Guest
Creative Director: Moira Clinch
Publisher: Paul Carslake

Color separation in Singapore by
PICA Digital Pte Ltd
Printed in China by
1010 Printing International Ltd

First U.S. Edition: April 2011

10 9 8 7 6 5 4 3 2 1

Introduction

Traditional patchwork quilts are objects of great beauty, but take considerable time to make. Today's quilter enjoys tackling smaller projects, such as tote bags, wall hangings, pillows, and other home and personal accessories. Mini-block designs, measuring 5in (12.7cm), 4½in (11.4cm), 4in (10.2cm), and 3in (7.6cm) square, are just the right size to bring visual variety and interest to these little treasures.

This book brings 130 gorgeous little blocks together, including new designs and traditional favorites, in ten chapters themed around block styles. Each block is accompanied by a photograph, cutting list, diagram, icons to indicate technique and skill level, and full instructions (templates, where used, are given full size, starting on page 118). There are mix and match illustrations with plenty of ideas for different block combinations for small quilts, pillows, and wall hangings, plus five easy projects. Select the blocks you want to make from the illustrated contents on pages 4–7.

These mini-blocks don't use a lot of fabric so you can make the most of the latest coordinated packs of strips, squares, or smaller pieces, which give you an entire range in one pack and mean that you don't have to buy a lot of

Fabric packs
Strip cuts (above) are made by many manufacturers. Charm packs (left) are available in coordinating stripes and plains.

different yardage. They are also ideal for using up your scraps. A guide to selecting fabrics is given on pages 16–17. You can, of course, combine blocks from various chapters if you wish, coordinating them easily by using the same fabric selection and adding borders, as described on page 26.

Patchwork and appliqué techniques used to make the blocks are clearly

explained with step-by-step photographs, from cutting out to finishing off. There is information on how to layer and quilt your project, including how to bind the edges where appropriate and how to add a hanging sleeve (see page 30). This section also includes information about how to use differently sized blocks in a sampler project—you might want to use all the blocks for a really large quilt!

▶ **Potholder**
A country-style block forms the center of this potholder on page 109.

◀ **Mini tote bag**
This bag, on page 51, combines three different blocks.

▶ **Brooches**
The brooches on page 67 use just a single block each.

▼ **Book bag**
Carry a special book in the pretty bag on page 99.

Block themes and chapters

You can make these blocks in other fabrics of your choice—the combination of block and fabrics used is just a suggestion, so you can be as creative and original as you wish.

Almost Amish, page 36
Miniature versions of the famous traditional quilts made by the Amish community, in rich, plain colors.

Crazy Colors, page 76
Contemporary irregular piecing is made easy with these colorful designs in a myriad of glowing batiks.

Retro Revival, page 44
Designs reflecting mid-century modern style, perfect for retro fabrics that combine natural textures with minimalist motifs.

Taupe Tranquillity, page 84
Revisit some of the cutest blocks with cool taupe colors and quirky prints for a timeless handmade vibe.

Thrifty Thirties, page 52
Original thirties' favorites are combined with Art Deco inspirations—just the thing for repro thirties fabrics.

Japanese Odyssey, page 92
Bold colors and sparkling golden metallic prints celebrate the sights and patterns of Japan.

Stars and Pinwheels, page 60
Show your quilting sparkle with some heavenly piecing, or put your blocks in a spin with pinwheels in chalky primary colors.

Country Classics, page 100
Red and green country fabrics are perfect for these traditional blocks interpreted with homestead style.

English Traditions, page 68
Simple blocks made by eighteenth-century quilters are brought up to date with gentle "shabby chic" prints and pastel shades.

Log Cabin, page 110
Strip patchwork explores the treasury of Log Cabin block designs, in a fresh springtime palette that brings the blocks right up to date.

About This Book

The illustrated contents list at the beginning of the book shows all the blocks together. Use it to find the blocks you like and as the starting point for your quilt or project design.

Techniques

This section has detailed information on equipment and techniques, including photographs showing how to construct the blocks. At the end, there is information on how to make simple projects such as a pillow, table runners, and wall hangings, plus how to finish a quilt, from putting the blocks together to basic quilting and binding.

Step-by-steps

All of the techniques required to make the blocks are explained step-by-step.

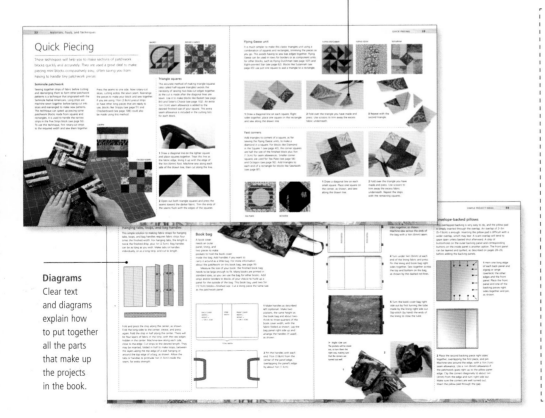

Diagrams

Clear text and diagrams explain how to put together all the parts that make up the projects in the book.

Understanding the symbols

Every block design has at-a-glance symbols indicating the skill level and technique.

SKILL LEVEL

 EASY

 INTERMEDIATE

ADVANCED

TECHNIQUE

 PATCHWORK

 APPLIQUÉ

Note: The patchwork and appliqué symbols together indicate that the block is made using a combination of both techniques.

Block size

When sewn together, the finished sizes of the blocks are:

5in (12.7cm),

4½in (11.4cm)

4in (10.2cm)

3in (7.6cm)

Thus the actual size of the individual blocks is ½in (1.3cm) larger. Take care with your seam allowances when piecing narrow strips or small patches, so all your blocks measure the correct size when finished. Taking fractionally larger seam allowances on blocks with many pieces will gradually reduce the size of the block. Blocks of different sizes can have borders added to increase the size and enable you to use them together in simple square sets. Alternatively, you can combine them in medallion or strip arrangements, using different sizes.

Block directory

This main part of the book contains all the cutting and construction information for each block, with a photograph, fabric selection, cutting list, construction method, and at-a-glance symbols giving more information. Follow either imperial or metric measurements throughout—do not switch between the two. Remember that the patchwork cutting list specifications include ¼in (6mm) seam allowances.

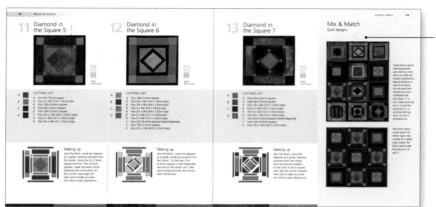

Mix & Match

Mix and match ideas for combining blocks in different layouts appear throughout the directory. Use them to help plan your project, changing blocks as you wish. Alternatively, you can make a mix and match or a project exactly as it is.

Cutting lists

Each block is accompanied by a list, showing the fabric used and the sizes of the fabric pieces required to make the block.

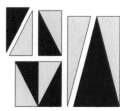

Mini projects

An assortment of smaller projects appears throughout the book (a mini tote bag, a pincushion, brooches, a book bag, and a potholder) plus there are more ideas in the Techniques section.

Exploded block diagrams

These diagrams illustrate how to make each block and the order in which you should piece the patches together.

Templates

Templates are provided for all blocks that require them. They are shown full size, so you can simply trace or photocopy them.

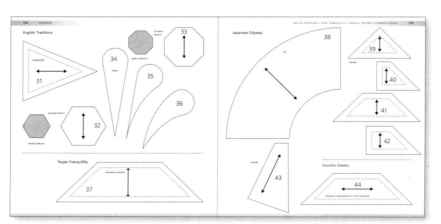

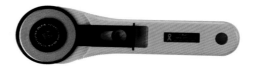

Materials, Tools, and Techniques

In this section you will find all you need to get started, from choosing fabrics to the techniques needed to make the blocks, plus numerous design ideas. An overview of equipment will help you gather together all you need. Finally, there are techniques and tips for completing your project.

◀ **Snail Trail**
Block 17, Snail Trail, from page 46, shown actual size.

Equipment

If you are already a quilter, you will have most of the necessary tools and materials for making your blocks and quilts. If not, this checklist covers the specialist tools you'll need, in addition to your regular sewing equipment.

COTON À BRODER THREAD

HAND-QUILTING THREAD

THREAD FOR PIECING

VARIEGATED PERLE THREAD

THREAD SNIPS

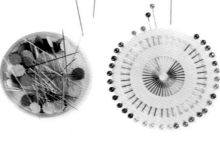

Scissors

Use fabric scissors for cutting fabric, embroidery scissors for cutting threads, and paper scissors for cutting paper templates.

Pins and safety pins

Select fine pins, such as good-quality dressmaking pins or silk pins, for piecing patchwork. Flower pins have a flat head so they don't twist on the fabric. Safety pins can be used instead of basting to hold the quilt layers together for quilting.

Threads for machine and hand sewing

Medium thickness (50) cotton sewing thread is best for piecing. Choose neutral colors that blend with your fabrics. Thicker (30 or 40) cotton thread can also be used for machine- or hand-quilting. Special quilting threads include variegated threads and metallic threads.

Hand-quilting threads are treated for smooth hand sewing. Other threads can be treated with beeswax or silicone wax to resist knotting—pull the thread over the edge of the wax block several times. Embroidery threads, including perle no. 12 and *coton à broder*, can be used for big-stitch quilting (see page 29).

Needles for hand sewing

Sharps (general hand-sewing needles) or a special appliqué needle can be used for hand appliqué (see page 25), where a longer needle is useful. Betweens are specialist hand-quilting needles, but smaller sharps can also be used.

Needles for machine sewing

Universal needles, in size 10–12 (USA) or size 70 or 80 (European), are good for machine sewing. Quilting needles are sharper and best for machine quilting. Try Microtex for finer fabrics. For quilting with metallic threads, use a Metallica needle with a longer, harder eye to prevent threads snapping.

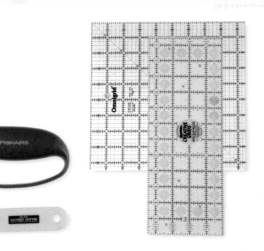
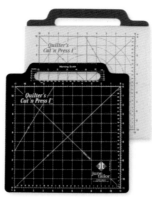
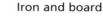
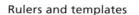

Iron and board

An ordinary iron and board are fine for pressing blocks. Use the appropriate temperature setting and avoid steaming blocks excessively, as this can distort the patchwork. A small travel iron or a mini appliqué iron is best for ironing on bias tape. A pressing mat or small ironing board is convenient to use near your sewing machine.

Sewing machine

Useful features for patchwork and quilting include a good straight stitch and a "needle down" option. A ¼in (6mm) patchwork foot is essential for accurate patchwork. If you want to machine-quilt your patchwork, a walking foot (for straight lines) and a darning foot (also called an embroidery foot or quilting foot, for free motion quilting) will be necessary. A large space under the machine arm will allow for easier machine quilting, but smaller projects are quite easy to handle on the machine.

Rotary cutter

A cutter with a 28mm or 45mm blade will be most useful (blades are sold in metric sizes only). Try out several cutters to find one that suits your hand best. The blades are razor-sharp, so always replace the blade guard after cutting and never leave the cutter where children or pets can reach it. The cutter must be used with a mat.

Cutting mat

A large mat is best—an A2 (16½ × 23⅜in 420 × 594mm) mat is a good size for general patchwork cutting. If you are going to work with charm packs, ready-cut strips, or larger precut squares, a smaller A3 (11¾ x 16½/297 × 420mm) mat is fine. Choose a mat with a printed grid, either imperial or metric, depending which measuring system you prefer.

Rulers and templates

Rulers are made in many different shapes and sizes. A rectangular ruler up to about 14in (35cm) long and 4½in (11.4cm) wide with 60-degree and 45-degree markings is a good choice. A wider ruler, 6in (15.2cm) or 6½in (16.5cm) long, is good for squaring up finished blocks. Look at the line markings and choose colors that you will be able to see against your fabric. Use the same make of ruler whenever possible, as measurements can vary slightly between manufacturers and between the ruler and mat. Double-check before cutting. Circle templates are used for several blocks, or make your own from card or template plastic. Use the appropriate size of circle template to cut circles as required for blocks.

Marking pens and pencils

Use erasable pens and pencils to mark around templates and to mark guidelines for quilting. Always follow the manufacturer's instructions, because what removes some marks will set others permanently.

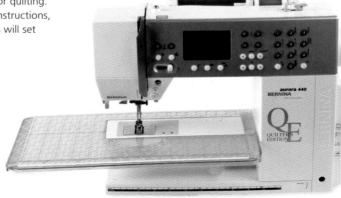

Selecting Fabrics

Fabric strips
Strips (right, far right, and below right) are usually sold as rolls, and may be combined with coordinating squares.

Mini blocks and smaller projects don't require lots of yardage to make. Ready-cut packs of strips, squares, and other pieces make coordinating fabrics super-simple. Look out for fabric ranges that suit your style, possibly adding 1yd (1m) or a fat quarter to bring it all together, or go through your scrap bag for smaller pieces.

Both fabric manufacturers and quilt stores package various special fabric cuts aimed at taking any difficulties out of coordinating fabrics. Packs made by manufacturers are often coordinated around one fabric range and may contain every print (typically up to 40 different fabrics or more), while stores may mix and match across several ranges. Manufacturers typically give their various cuts a nifty but copyrighted name, so the names of these packs vary, depending on the company that packed them; look for the fabric size on the label so you know what you are buying. Buying fabric packaged to go takes the hassle out of selecting and coordinating fabrics yourself, plus you will have a larger variety of fabric patterns for your money. The fabrics used in each chapter are mentioned in the chapter introduction.

Square packs

Smaller squares have been known as "charms" for a long time. Typically, the size varies from 4in (10.2cm) to 7in (17.8cm), depending on whose charm pack you are using. Most manufacturers seem to have settled on 5in (12.7cm) as their ideal charm size, with anything up to 40 different fabrics in the pack (some may be duplicated or have near duplicates, which can be useful). Stores may have fewer charms in a pack but offer a larger selection of sizes. One of the most popular larger square sizes is 10in (25.4cm). Again, fabric manufacturers tend to include an entire range, while stores may offer two of each print, carefully coordinated by their design staff. This is the most useful fabric cut for mini blocks, giving a large variety of prints but allowing both strips and squares to be cut with ease and little wastage.

► **Fabric squares**
Squares measuring 10in (25.4cm) and 5in (12.7cm) offer a convenient way of purchasing fabric.

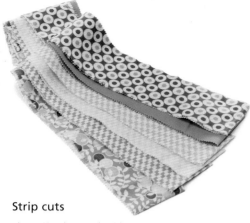

Strip cuts

The 2½in- (6.4cm-) wide strip cut has become standard for many fabric manufacturers and stores. The strips are cut across the fabric width, selvage to selvage, most frequently sold rolled up and tied with a ribbon. They are good for blocks that require strips or pieces where one measurement is no larger than 2½in (6.4cm).

A narrower 1½in (3.8cm) strip is also available from some fabric manufacturers, with the same number of strips as the 2½in- (6.4cm-) wide roll. These are less versatile, but could be a good choice if you are making blocks with lots of 1½in (3.8cm) squares or 1½in- (3.8cm-) wide strips. Wider strip cuts, up to 5in (12.7cm), are sometimes available, and can be used for many differently sized patchwork pieces. These wider strips usually have far fewer fabrics in a roll, with ten or twelve being typical.

Pinked edges

Several manufacturers cut their square and strip packs with a minute zigzagged (pinked) edge, to stop the fabric packs fraying when handled. Check the measurement across the strip or square before starting to cut, as some take the outer points of the pinked edge into the measurement and some don't. The pinked edge doesn't need to be cut off and can be incorporated into your ¼in (6mm) seam allowance. The pinking can make quite a lot of fluff along the edge of a roll or square pack, so dust off the edges before taking it into your sewing area.

Scrap bags

There's something irresistible about a scrap collection. Some fabric manufacturers have started packaging the scraps from their strip production into scrap bags, and quilt stores have been selling scrap bags for years. Of course, the fabric sizes will be irregular, but there will be a good selection suitable for mini-blocks. You can also delve into your own scrap bag or arrange a scrap swap with quilting friends—it is easiest to do this by weight, agreeing to swap, say, 8oz (250g) of fabric.

Cuts from yardage

Fat quarters, eighths, and packs of smaller rectangular pieces have been around for a while. A "fat" quarter—considered almost the fabric currency standard in the quilt world!—is a yard (or about a meter) quartered by cutting vertically and horizontally, as opposed to a "thin" quarter, which is only cut across the bolt. An eighth is half a fat quarter. All these cuts are based on a yard (or meter) of fabric that is approximately 42–44in (107–110cm) wide, the standard width for quilting fabrics. They are popular cuts for stores, but some manufacturers also prepare their own precut packs.

Smaller cuts, such as 9 × 11in (22.9 × 27.9cm), are also available, sometimes sold as appliqué packs. Once again, different manufacturers and stores may have their own names for these, so check the actual fabric sizes.

▼ **Fat quarter bundles**
These offer larger pieces from a coordinated range.

Cutting Fabrics

Rotary-cutting the fabrics for your blocks is more accurate than using scissors. It can also be quicker because you can cut through more than one fabric layer at a time (see Crazy Colors, pages 76–77). Some blocks require pieces to be cut from templates, but rotary cutting is used wherever possible. All patchwork templates include a ¼in (6mm) seam allowance. Make cutting out easier by pressing your fabric smooth before you start.

Strips

With the ruler firmly on top of your fabric, square off uneven ends and cut off the tightly woven selvage. Fold the fabric if required, and line up the relevant measurement on the ruler with the straight edge of the fabric. Place the rotary cutter against the ruler's edge and cut. Right-handed people will use the cutter to the left of the ruler; left-handed people will use the cutter on the right of the ruler. Cut with the straight grain of the fabric where possible; with printed stripes and checkered prints, cut with the pattern, unless you want an off-grain effect.

Squares and rectangles

Cut strips into squares and rectangles by aligning the ruler in the same way as before and cutting across the strip of fabric. Where cutting lists specify "halved" or "quartered diagonally," this means "cut diagonally."

Cutting safety

The rotary cutter has a very sharp blade and it is easy to cut yourself or others accidentally. Always take the following precautions when using your cutter:

- Hold the cutter firmly at a 45-degree angle in the same hand that you use for writing, and hold the ruler in place with your other hand.

- Cut with the blade against the side of your ruler—on the right if you are right-handed and on the left if you are left-handed. The patchwork piece you are cutting is under the ruler.

- Use a sharp blade that is free from nicks and other damage—a dull blade requires more pressure when you cut and risks the blade slipping.

- Stand up to cut if you can, and place the mat on a firm surface—a kitchen counter or sturdy table is ideal.

- Always cut away from yourself.

- Always replace the safety guard on the cutter—make a habit of doing this after every cut.

- Wear something on your feet when you cut, in case you drop the cutter.

- Keep cutting equipment away from children and pets.

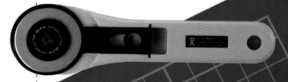

Triangles from squares

Cut along one diagonal to make a half-square triangle, lining up the 45-degree angle on your ruler with the edge of the square.

Cut again for quarter-square triangles. Some half-square triangle units used in blocks are made with the triangle square method shown on page 22.

Rotary cutting with templates

Straight-sided shapes can be cut using templates and a ruler for perfectly straight edges. Trace off or copy the relevant template from the templates section (see pages 118–125) and cut out. Pin the template to the fabric with flat-headed or small-headed pins, line the ruler up with the template edge, and cut.

Photocopying templates

The copying process can stretch and distort templates by up to 2 percent lengthwise, spoiling the accuracy of the template, although some photocopiers are more accurate than others. This isn't a problem for appliqué, but check any photocopied templates you plan to use for patchwork.

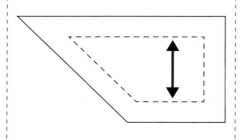

Cutting appliqué pieces

Trace off or copy the relevant template from the templates section (see pages 118–125) and cut out. Pin the template to the fabric and draw around it with a fabric marker. Cut the piece out with scissors, carefully following the drawn line.

Basic Piecing

Machine-sewn patchwork for mini blocks is quick to do. Shorten the length of the machine stitch to around two-thirds the normal length—that is, around 12–14 stitches per inch (about 1.7–2mm long). If you prefer hand piecing, draw a guideline in pencil, use very small running stitches with an occasional backstitch, and start and finish with several backstitches and a knot. Whichever method you choose, use a ¼in (6mm) seam allowance throughout. For clarity, contrasting threads have been used in some photographs.

Chain piecing

Chain piecing speeds up sewing patchwork. When you have sewn your first two pieces together, don't cut the thread. Place the next two pieces together and sew them a stitch or two after the first two pieces. Continue like this to make a "chain," which can be cut up afterward.

Laying out the block

Lay out the pieces before you begin sewing, and join them together following the individual block instructions. Many blocks require pieces to be sewn together in rows first. Arranging the block helps you to avoid sewing pieces together in the wrong order.

Machine piecing

Place the first two pieces right sides together, making sure the edges to be sewn line up. Align the fabric edges with the edge of the ¼in (6mm) foot and sew the seam. It may help if you sit slightly to the right of the machine needle so you can see this easily. Use a fabric scrap as a "leader," so the first patchwork stitches do not get chewed up. Pin longer seams at right angles to the stitching line and remove pins as you sew.

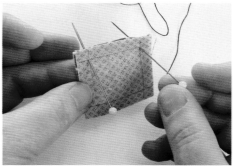

Hand piecing (American method)

Many American quilters hand-piece their patchwork. The stitching lines need to be marked ¼in (6mm) from the edge of each piece, as shown. Align the pieces to be sewn by pushing a pin through each end of the stitching line on the first piece. Line up the second piece underneath, right sides together, and push the pins through the ends of the line on that piece too. With the fabrics close together, insert more pins to secure the seam for sewing. Sew seams with running stitch, as detailed above.

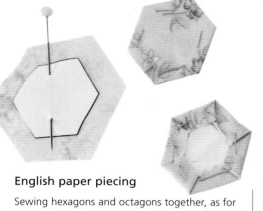

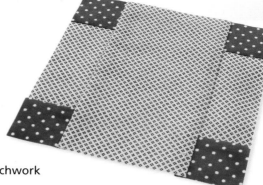

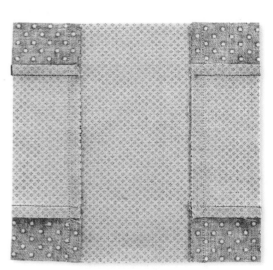

◀ **Pressing seams**
Pressing your patchwork as you go along will ensure a neater and better finish.

English paper piecing

Sewing hexagons and octagons together, as for Hexagon Rosette and Octagon Rosette (see page 74), is easiest with English paper piecing. Cut paper templates to the exact finished size of each piece and baste the fabric patches around them, sewing through the paper. Right sides together, oversew or whipstitch the pieces together, starting and finishing with a knot, about ¼in (6mm) from the corner of the patch. Press when complete and remove the papers.

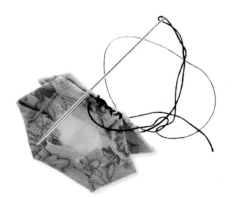

Pressing patchwork

Press each stage of your patchwork as you go along, with the seam allowance to one side; this will help to keep the batting from "bearding" or coming through the seam later. Begin pressing from the right side of the block to avoid a "lip" forming at the seam; you can turn it over and check the seam allowances afterward. Press toward the darker fabric out of preference, as pressing dark toward light can cause a shadow effect on paler fabrics. Pressing in alternate directions makes the seams interlock neatly, as shown. For blocks pieced from the center outward, such as the Log Cabin blocks (see pages 110–117), press seams toward the outside of the block. Press with a dry iron or just a little steam, using an up and down action so the patchwork is not stretched and distorted—you are pressing, not ironing. Good pressing can really make a difference to your patchwork, so get it right before you continue piecing.

Sewing tip

Replace the standard zigzag throat plate on your machine with a straight-stitch plate for patchwork and quilting. The needle cannot be accidentally dragged sideways, giving a better straight stitch. Consult your machine dealer for more information. Remember to replace the zigzag plate afterward!

▲ **Machine appliqué edge**
Stitches like blanket stitch need the zigzag throat plate.

Quick Piecing

These techniques will help you to make sections of patchwork blocks quickly and accurately. They are used a great deal to make piecing mini blocks comparatively easy, often saving you from having to handle tiny patchwork pieces.

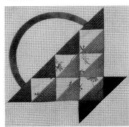

BASKET

SISTER'S CHOICE

Seminole patchwork

Sewing together strips of fabric before cutting and rearranging them to form other patchwork patterns is a technique that originated with the Seminole Native Americans. Long strips are machine-sewn together before being cut into slices and rearranged to make new patterns. This technique can speed up piecing some patchwork blocks made from squares and rectangles. It is used to handle the narrow strips in the Five Strips block (see page 93). To use this technique, first rotary-cut strips to the required width and sew them together.

Press the seams to one side. Now rotary-cut slices, cutting across the sewn seam. Rearrange the pieces to make your block and sew together. If you are using 1½in (3.8cm) precut strips or have other long pieces that are ready to use, blocks like Strippy (see page 51) and Checkerboard (see page 108) could also be made using this method.

Triangle squares

This accurate method of making triangle squares (also called half-square triangles) avoids the necessity of sewing two bias-cut edges together, as the cut is made after the diagonal lines are sewn. Use it to make blocks like Basket (see page 84) and Sister's Choice (see page 102). An extra ⅜in (1cm) seam allowance is added to the desired finished size of your square. This extra seam allowance is included in the cutting lists for each block.

STRIPPY

CHECKERBOARD

1 Draw a diagonal line on the lighter square and place squares together. Treat this line as the fabric edge, lining it up with the edge of the ¼in (6mm) foot. Machine-sew along each side of the drawn line, then cut along the line.

2 Open out both triangle squares and press the seams toward the darker fabric. Trim the ends of the seams flush with the edges of the squares.

Flying Geese unit

It is much simpler to make this classic triangles unit using a combination of squares and rectangles, trimming the pieces as you go. This avoids having to sew bias edges together. Flying Geese can be used in rows for borders or as component units for other blocks, such as Flying Dutchman (see page 107) and Eight-pointed Star (see page 62). Blocks like Suzannah (see page 65) use just one square to add a triangle to a rectangle.

FLYING DUTCHMAN

FLYING GEESE

SUZANNAH

1 Draw a diagonal line on each square. Right sides together, place one square on the rectangle and sew along the drawn line.

2 Fold over the triangle you have made and press. Use scissors to trim away the excess fabric underneath.

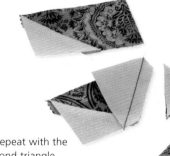

3 Repeat with the second triangle.

Fast corners

Add triangles to corners of a square, as for sewing the Flying Geese units, to make a diamond in a square. For blocks like Diamond in the Square 1 (see page 40), the corner squares are half the size of the finished block plus ½in (1.3cm) for seam allowances. Smaller corner squares are used for Tea Plate (see page 56) and Octagon (see page 92). Add triangles to each end of a rectangle for blocks like Sawtooth (see page 87).

1 Draw a diagonal line on each small square. Place one square on the corner, as shown, and sew along the drawn line.

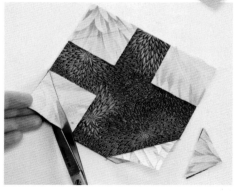

2 Fold over the triangle you have made and press. Use scissors to trim away the excess fabric underneath. Repeat the steps with the remaining squares.

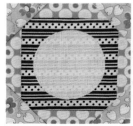

TEA PLATE   **OCTAGON**

Crazy Patchwork and Appliqué

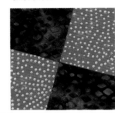

CRISSCROSS

Both these techniques add a different look to your quilt blocks. Crazy patchwork is usually sewn to a foundation square, using a stitch-and-flip method, and is a form of appliqué. Random patchwork methods, which go well with crazy patchwork, are included here. Other simple appliqué methods are used where they were the easiest way to make the block.

Crazy patchwork

Constructing crazy patchwork by machine, using the stitch and flip method, is quick and easy to do. There is no need to cut strips to a regular length, and wedge shapes and irregular strips can be used up. It is used for the Triangular Strips and Random Rosette blocks (see pages 82 and 83). See individual block instructions for more information.

Random Rosette

For the Random Rosette, start with a square of muslin and pin the first piece to the center right, right side up. Pin another piece to this, face down and overlapping one of the edges of the center piece by at least ¼in (6mm). Sew, and flip the piece over. Repeat with more strips, working outward until the muslin is covered.

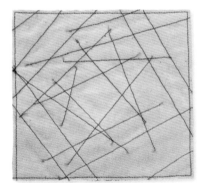

Triangular Strips

The Triangular Strips block allows the background square to be part of the front of the finished block. Starting on the center diagonal, strips are sewn and flipped toward the corner.

SPINNING SQUARE   RANDOM NINE PATCH

Random patchwork effects

Stacking up squares of different fabrics and cutting through all the layers at various angles, without necessarily measuring the pieces, can create exciting contemporary effects. Blocks like Random Nine Patch, Random Square (see page 81) and Spinning Square (see page 82) are made this way. The number of squares usually relates to the number of pieces in the block, so you have a number of identically shaped pieces, each from one of the fabrics. Blocks may also be made by cutting at random and rejoining the pieces with a 1in- (2.5cm-) wide strip, as in Crisscross (see page 77).

1 Layer up the number of squares as required for the block. The outside edges don't have to be perfectly aligned, as the finished blocks are trimmed to size. Cut slices through the block, as described in the individual block instructions. The block shown here is Layered Wedges (see page 79).

2 Take one piece of each fabric and lay out the block before piecing, following the block instructions.

Uneven edges
The edges of the pieces often don't line up and the block is trimmed to the desired size. Blocks are made in sets of the same number as the number of starting squares.

Appliqué

Appliqué is made by layering and stitching fabric pieces to a background to make a design. There are a small number of blocks in this book where appliqué was the easiest technique to create the design. Some blocks, such as Winding Ways (see page 49) are usually made in patchwork, but appliqué avoids tricky curved piecing. Fused (also called bonded) appliqué can be edged with machine stitching.

Using the templates

The templates on pages 118–125 are shown actual size. The template reference number and page number are given in the block cutting list. A few templates are used in more than one block; the number relates to the first block where they are used. Trace off or photocopy the templates you need for your block. Pin the templates to the fabric and draw around the edge of the paper with a contrasting fabric marker or pencil. Cut the pieces out. Some templates have a ¼in (6mm) turning allowance as required by the design.

Hemmed appliqué

Blocks like Moon over Mountain and Kimono (see page 96) use appliqué with a turned hem. Following the individual block instructions, fold under and press ¼in (6mm) along the side of the appliqué piece, as directed. Pin the appliqué to the background piece and sew to the background. Hand-sew with small appliqué stitches, coming up through the folded edge and down through the background fabric before taking the next stitch. Some sewing machines have an invisible appliqué stitch feature which may be used instead.

MOON OVER MOUNTAIN

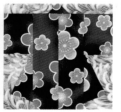

KIMONO

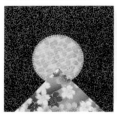

PLUME

Fused appliqué

A very quick appliqué method involves ironing fusible webbing to the back of the fabric, cutting out the pieces, and ironing them onto a backing fabric. The appliqué shapes need to be traced as mirror images onto the back of the fusible web paper. The appliqué pieces need no turning allowance. The edges are best stitched with a machine satin, zigzag, or blanket stitch, as the fusible webbing stiffens the fabrics, making hand sewing difficult.

BASKET

Fusible bias tape

Ready-made ¼in- (6mm-) wide fusible bias tape is quick and easy to use. It is made in various colors, including variegated shades. It is used to make the handle for Basket (see page 84) but could also be used for a different handle on Teacup (see page 56), or as a substitute for piecing on Torii (see page 97).

Following the manufacturer's instructions, iron the bias tape in place, then sew down the edges with small stitches, as for hemmed appliqué. Depending on the block construction, ends of tapes are sewn into patchwork seams or can be covered with other pieces of bias tape (if making a variation on the Torii block).

Patchwork Quilt Ideas

Blocks can be arranged or "set" in various ways for different little quilt designs. You may wish to decide your block layout at the beginning of your project or make several blocks and take the design from there. Sketching a plan of your project on squared paper will help. Sew blocks together in rows and sew the rows together to complete your quilt top.

Sampler quilt

Making just one of each block in a quilt is called a sampler. Same-size blocks can be sewn straight together if you wish, which usually works best if you have been very color-coordinated with your blocks.

Adding borders

This book includes 3in (7.6cm), 4in (10.2cm), 4½in (11.4cm), and 5in (12.7cm) blocks (finished sizes). If you want to combine blocks from different chapters, you may need to add borders to make all the blocks the same size. The diagram below shows the size of border you will need to enlarge the blocks in the left-hand column to make them compatible with the blocks along the top.

FINISHED BLOCK SIZE TO BE ENLARGED	FINISHED BLOCK SIZE TO MATCH		
	4in (10.2cm)	4½in (11.4cm)	5in (12.7cm)
3in (7.6cm)	3½ x 1in (8.9 x 2.5cm) 4½ x 1 in (11.4 x 2.5cm)	3½ x 1¼in (8.9 x 3.2cm) 5 x 1¼in (12.7 x 3.2cm)	3½ x 1½in (8.9 x 3.8cm) 5½ x 1½in (14 x 3.8cm)
4in (10.2cm)		4½ x ¾in (11.4 x 1.9cm) 5 x ¾in (12.7 x 1.9cm)	4½ x 1 in (11.4 x 2.5cm) 5½ x 1 in (14 x 2.5cm)
4½in (11.4cm)			5 x ¾in (12.7 x 1.9cm) 5½ x ¾in (14 x 1.9cm)

You will need two borders in each size, for opposite sides of each block that is being enlarged. The sizes given include ¼in (6mm) seam allowances.

Checkerboard

Alternating various pairs of blocks with just two pieced designs produces a checkerboard effect. Alternating patchwork or appliqué blocks with unpieced squares makes more complex blocks that cover a larger area without too much extra effort.

On-point settings

Many blocks, such as Basket (see page 84) and Cake Stand (see page 85), work well set on a 45-degree angle. This can make the overall design of the quilt more lively and add interest to the blocks. The blocks are still sewn together in rows, but diagonally, with a half- or quarter-block triangle at each end. For side triangles, cut squares ¾in (1.9cm) larger than the total block size, i.e., 6½in (16.5cm) for a 5in (12.7cm) finished block size, and quarter diagonally. For corner triangles, cut squares half the size of the finished block, plus ⅞in (2.2cm), i.e., 2⅞in (7.3cm) where the finished block is 5in (12.7cm), and halve diagonally.

Sashing

Sashing refers to strips inserted between the quilt blocks. It separates them visually, as well as separating the construction seams from one block to the next. It can be a good place to introduce a touch of color. Sashing can help bring a sense of unity to blocks made with different fabrics. Smaller squares added to the sashing at the corners of the blocks, called posts, allow the sashing strips to be the same length as the block sides.

Medallion quilts with different block sizes

Medallion arrangements are another way to combine differently sized blocks. Plan your quilt on graph paper before you start and combine blocks in multiples of block sizes and numbers of blocks: five 3in (7.6cm) blocks will fit with three 5in (12.7cm) blocks, for example. The same principle can be used to create quilts where blocks are arranged in rows or columns.

One-of-a-kind and asymmetric designs

A one-of-a-kind quilt needs planning to achieve an apparently random effect. Making a number of blocks and laying pieces out in various ways can be a good starting point if you like to work intuitively, adding pieces and squaring up patchwork as you go. Alternatively, plan out your unique quilt on graph paper first.

Quilting and Finishing

Once your patchwork is finished and the blocks sewn together, sandwiching the top, batting, and backing is the next step toward completing your quilt. An optional border can help frame your quilt blocks, whereas hand or machine quilting holds the layers together securely.

Adding a quilt border

To add a simple border, measure your patchwork vertically through the center (a), and cut two border pieces to that length. Pin the borders to the sides of your patchwork, lining up the ends and the center, and then ease the side of the patchwork to the border. Sew, and press the seams toward the border strips. For the top and bottom borders, measure across the total sewn width of your patchwork square and side borders (b). Measuring through the center each time is more accurate than measuring along the patchwork edge. A series of narrow and wide borders can be added the same way. Quilt borders can be whatever width you like and blocks can be bordered individually too. The border can also be made from patchwork, with a narrow inner border between it and the blocks.

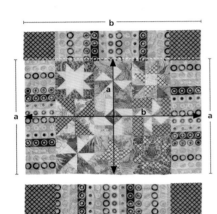

CORNER SQUARES MAKE UP WIDTH ON TOP AND BOTTOM BORDERS

Batting and basting

Choose an appropriate batting for your quilting technique (your quilt store will be able to advise you). Puffy polyester battings give dimension to appliqué blocks, but cotton and cotton/polyester blends are better for machine quilting. The backing fabric and batting should be about 2in (5cm) larger than the quilt top all around. If the backing is pieced, use a ½in (1.3cm) seam and press the seams open. Press the fabrics and smooth out the backing on a flat, clean surface, covering any important tabletops

with heavy cardboard or wood sheet. Hold the backing edges down at intervals with masking tape. Spread the batting on top and smooth out. Repeat with the quilt top, making sure the corners are square. Starting at the center, baste the layers together. You may wish to pin the layers with dressmaking pins or omit the hand basting and baste with safety pins instead. Using a teaspoon to lever up the point of the needle after each stitch prevents your fingers getting sore.

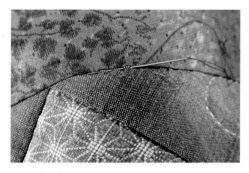

Bagging out without a binding

The quilt top, backing, and batting will be basted together in a different order before quilting, so decide if you want to use this finishing method before making the quilt sandwich. It is the method used for the Brooches on page 67.

Place the batting on the wrong side of the backing fabric, as if making a quilt sandwich with only two layers, spreading the batting out, and laying the backing face up onto it. For larger pieces, the layers will need to be basted with stitches rather than pins, which tend to catch on each other when turning the quilt right side out. Lay the quilt top over the backing and batting sandwich, right sides together with the backing, and smooth it out. Pin and machine-sew all around, using a ¼in (6mm) seam allowance, and leaving a gap unsewn at the bottom of the quilt. The whole quilt will be turned right side out through this gap, so don't make it too small. Trim the backing to the same size as the quilt. Trim the excess batting from the seam allowance and across the gap. Clip the corners (as described above) and "bag out," turning the quilt right side out through the unsewn gap. Smooth the top over the batting and backing, baste the layers together before quilting, and slip-stitch the gap closed when complete.

Hand-sewing around the edge makes a crisp finish on larger pieces. Work from the back, taking a short running stitch through the backing and a longer running stitch through the seam allowance inside the edge, about ⅛in (3mm) from the edge. Don't let the stitching show on the quilt front.

Hand quilting

Smaller projects may be easier to quilt without a frame, but use a hoop to quilt if you prefer, basting pieces of scrap fabric to the edges of your quilt so it is large enough to fasten into the hoop. Whichever method you use, begin quilting from the center, or quilt in a grid along the seam lines in the ditch between blocks or sashing, quilting block details later. Use quilting thread slightly darker than your fabric. To hand-quilt, start by tying two small knots at the end of the quilting thread.

From the front of the quilt, take long stitches in the opposite direction to the way you will quilt and pop the two knots through the fabric and batting. With your non-sewing hand under the quilt, take small running stitches in a rocking motion, going through all the layers. Feel the needle point emerging under the quilt and immediately push the point up again, taking several stitches before pulling the needle through. Using a thimble on each index finger will protect them. When the thread is finished, turn the quilt over and tie two more knots, popping these through the backing and into the quilt.

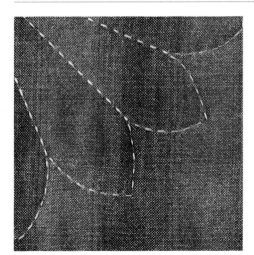

Big stitch and buttons

Giving a similar effect to traditional Japanese sashiko, big stitch uses thicker thread and is intended to be seen. Use it to add decorative quilting designs to your quilt. Threads like perle no. 12, fine sashiko thread, and *coton à broder* are all suitable. You can also use buttons to tie the quilt at intervals. Stitch through each button individually several times, right through the quilt layers.

Machine quilting

Machine quilting has a stronger linear effect than hand quilting. Start and finish at the edge of the piece if you can, to avoid having to sew in the thread ends afterward. Continuous line patterns are easiest to quilt. Turning a small project on the machine is very easy, so the walking foot can be used to quilt zigzags and other sharp turns in a design.

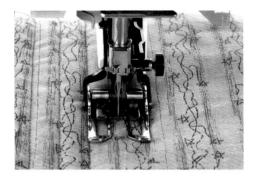

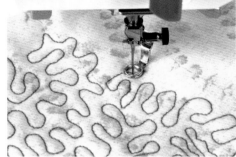

1 Use a walking foot on the machine to feed the layers of the quilt sandwich through at the same rate, preventing puckering. Use it for quilting straight lines, in the ditch or with a small gap around motifs, for grids, parallel lines, and gentle curves. With a zigzag throat plate on the machine, you can quilt any embroidery stitches your machine has installed.

2 Free-motion quilting requires a darning, quilting, or embroidery foot. With the machine feed dogs set in the down position, guide the quilt through the machine, moving the quilt in any direction, but evenly to maintain a consistent stitch length. Practice on smaller pieces before attempting a larger quilt.

Binding

The quilt can be bound with strips cut from coordinating fabric. These can be cut on the straight grain or on the bias. If you need to join strips for binding, press the joining seams open to reduce bulk and consider joining with a mitered seam.

Trim the backing and batting to match the edge of the quilt top. Baste or sew all around the top, close to the edge, to hold the layers together while applying the binding. Cut 1½in- (3.8cm-) wide binding strips, to the same length as the first edge to be bound and two 2in (5cm) longer than the remaining edges. Pin the first two strips to the corresponding quilt edges along the front of the quilt, setting the strip edge approximately ¼in (6mm) away from the quilt edge, and sew. Fold the binding around the edge, turn under a ¼in (6mm) allowance, and hem by hand with small stitches to the back of the quilt. Repeat for the two remaining edges, but allow the binding to overlap by 1in (2.5cm) at each end when machine sewing. Fold and sew these ends in before hemming the binding to the back of the quilt.

Making a hanging sleeve

To make a hanging sleeve for a rod or lathe at home, make sure the fabric tube will be wide enough to pass over any decorative finials or fasteners as well as the rod. Cut a strip of cotton twice the desired finished depth, adding on 2in (5cm) for a ½in (1.3cm) seam allowance, and as long as the width of the quilt. Turn under a small hem at each end. Fold the strip in half down its length and machine-sew into a tube. The seam will stay on the outside of the sleeve. Hand-sew the tube to the back of the quilt across the top and bottom edges, positioning the sleeve about ½in (1.3cm) from the top of the quilt. It should be invisible when the quilt is hung up. If you want to enter your quilt in a show, the hanging sleeve may need to be a certain width for the hanging system, so check with the organizers.

Simple Project Ideas

There are many ways that mini quilt blocks can be combined for smaller projects, including the mini tote bag, book bag, and pillows described here. Exact sizes are not given, as these will depend on which blocks you choose and whether you decide to add borders or sashing to the blocks (see page 27). Start and finish any construction seams with a few backstitches, for strength. Other projects are included in the Block Directory, on pages 67, 91, and 109.

Mini tote bag

Select several blocks and some coordinating fabric to make a mini tote bag. The sides of the bag can include any number of blocks you wish—the one in the Retro Revival chapter (see page 51) uses just three blocks, one of which is used in two halves, so each side of the bag has one and a half blocks. Using the outer bag panels as pattern pieces, bag linings can be easily constructed, whatever size you have made the bag. The bag is turned right side out through a gap left in the lining.

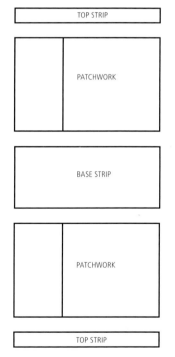

1 Sew the blocks together. Measure the total width of each patchwork panel and cut a base strip and two top strips the same length. The Retro Revival bag uses a 3½in- (8.9cm-) wide base strip and 1½in- (3.8cm-) wide top strips, but these can be wider if you wish. Sew these to the patchwork to make the bag panel, as shown. Layer and quilt the panel as desired (see Batting and basting, page 28). Use this completed bag panel as a pattern to cut a piece of fabric for the lining.

2 Fold the bag panel in half, right sides together, so it resembles the finished bag. Machine-sew the side seams. Do the same with the lining, but leave a 4in (10.2cm) gap unsewn in one side, to turn the finished bag right side out. Keeping both bag and lining inside out, fold the bottom corners to make a point, as shown. Mark a line at right angles to the seam, 1in (2.5cm) from the point, then pin and machine-sew across, creating a triangular flap of fabric. Cut off the flaps, about ½in (1.3cm) from the stitch line, and discard the scraps. This gives the bag a square base.

3IN (7.6CM)

3 Position the bag strap or handles on the top edge of the bag as required (see diagram). With the bag right side out and the lining inside out, place the bag inside the lining and align the top edges. Machine-sew around the top of the bag, sewing the lining to the outer bag all round with a ¼in (6mm) seam. Turn the bag right side out, through the unsewn gap in the lining side seam. Press the seam at the top of the bag. Machine- or hand-sew around the top of the bag, about ⅛in (3mm) from the edge. Turn the bag inside out and slip-stitch the gap in the lining closed.

Hanging tabs, loops, and bag handles

This simple solution to making fabric straps for hanging tabs, loops, and bag handles requires fabric strips four times the finished width. For hanging tabs, the length is twice the finished drop, plus 1in (2.5cm). Bag handles can be as long as you wish. Make tabs or handles individually, or as a long strip, and cut to length.

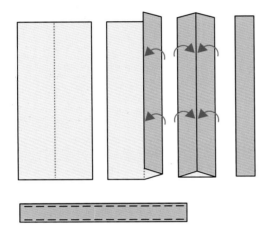

Fold and press the strip along the center, as shown. Fold the long sides to the center, crease, and press again. Fold the strip in half along the center. There will be four layers of fabric in the strip, with the raw edges hidden in the center. Machine-sew along each side, close to the edge. Cut strips to the desired length. They may be inserted, folded in half to make loops, between the layers along the top edge of a wall hanging or around the top edge of a bag, as shown. Allow the tabs or handles to protrude ½in (1.3cm) inside the seam, for extra strength.

Book bag

A book cover needs an outer panel, lining, and two pieces to make pockets to hold the book cover inside the bag. Add handles if you want to carry it around as a little bag. For more information about the patchwork on this book bag, see page 99.

Measure the size of your book: the finished book bag needs to be large enough to fit. Many books are printed in standard sizes, so you can use the bag for other books. Add strips and/or borders to blocks of your choice to build up a panel for the outside of the bag. This book bag used two 5in (12.7cm) blocks—finished size. Cut a lining piece the same size as the patchwork panel.

BACK COVER WIDTH = HEIGHT = + ½IN (1.3CM)	SPINE WIDTH	FRONT COVER WIDTH = HEIGHT = + ½IN (1.3CM)

TOTAL WIDTH

1 Make handles as described left (optional). Make two pockets, the same height as the book bag and about two-thirds to three-quarters of the book cover width, with the fabric folded as shown. Lay the bag panel right side up and arrange the handles (if used), as shown.

2 Pin the handles with each end 1½in (3.8cm) from the center of the panel edge, overlapping the panel's edge by about ½in (1.3cm).

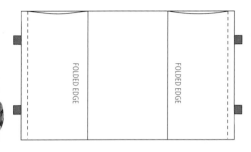

3 Place the folded pocket panels and bag panel right sides together, as shown. Machine-sew across the ends of the bag with a ¼in (6mm) seam.

4 Turn under ¼in (6mm) at each end of the lining fabric and press. Pin the lining and book bag right sides together. Sew together across the top and bottom on the bag, as shown by the dashed red lines.

5 Turn the book cover bag right side out by first turning the tube made by the lining right side out. Slip-stitch (by hand) the ends of the lining to close the tube.

▶ **Right side out**
The pockets will be inside out, so turn them the right way, making sure that the corners are turned out well.

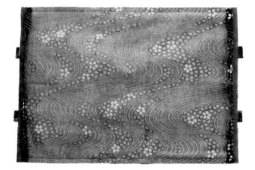

Envelope-backed pillows

This overlapped backing is very easy to do, and the pillow pad is simply inserted through the overlap. An overlap of 2–3in (5–7.6cm) is enough. Inserting the pillow pad is difficult with a wider overlap, which may tear. A scant overlap will tend to gape open unless basted shut afterward. A strip of buttonholes on the outer backing panel and corresponding buttons on the inside panel is another option. The front panel can be layered and quilted, as described on pages 28–29, before adding the backing panels.

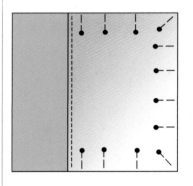

1 Hem one long edge of each back panel and zigzag or serge (overlock) the other edges and the front panel. Place the front panel and one of the backing pieces right sides together and pin, as shown.

2 Place the second backing piece right sides together, overlapping the first piece, and pin. Machine-sew around the edge, with a ⅜in (1cm) seam allowance. Use a ¼in (6mm) allowance if the patchwork goes right up to the pillow panel edge. Clip the corners diagonally to about ⅛in (3mm) from the edge and turn right side out. Make sure the corners are well turned out. Insert the pillow pad through the gap.

Block Directory

This directory includes all the cutting and construction information for every block, illustrated with photographs and diagrams, all arranged in ten themed chapters. Mix and match features give ideas for combining blocks and five mini projects suggest other ways to use the blocks. The possibilities for creative combinations are almost infinite, so have fun playing with the designs and making the blocks.

◄ **Pagoda**
Block 101, Pagoda, from
page 98, shown actual size.

Almost Amish

The quilts made by the Amish people, a religious community who settled in Pennsylvania from the eighteenth century, are very distinctive. The Amish are forbidden from using patterned textiles so their quilts are made only from plains, which are sometimes quite bright. Although they now use many other patchwork patterns, these blocks are based on the many variations of the medallion format typical of early Amish quilts. To add a subtle depth of color, hand-dyed fabrics, sold in packs of 9½in (24cm) squares, were used instead of flat plains, but you can use plain fabric if you prefer. A narrow border echoes the wide quilt bindings. Omit this border if you prefer 4½in (11.4cm) blocks.

1 Plain Quilt 1

[Size]
5in (12.7cm)

A ■
B ■
C ■

CUTTING LIST

A   One 2in (5cm) square
A   Two 5½ × ¾in (14 x 1.9cm) strips
A   Two 5 × ¾in (12.7 x 1.9cm) strips
B   Two 2 × 1in (5 x 2.5cm) strips
B   Two 3 × 1in (7.6 x 2.5cm) strips
C   Two 3 × 1½in (7.6 x 3.8cm) strips
C   Two 5 × 1½in (12.7 x 3.8cm) strips

Making up

Sew the block, using the diagram as a guide, working outward from the center. Take care to keep accurate ¼in (6mm) seam allowances.

2 Plain Quilt 2

[Size]
5in (12.7cm)

CUTTING LIST

A   One 3in (7.6cm) square
B   Two 3 × ¾in (7.6 x 1.9cm) strips
B   Two 3½ × ¾in (8.9 x 1.9cm) strips
B   Two 5 × ¾in (12.7 x 1.9cm) strips
B   Two 5½ × ¾in (14 x 1.9cm) strips
C   Two 3½ × 1¼in (8.9 x 3.2cm) strips
C   Two 5 × 1¼in (12.7 x 3.2cm) strips

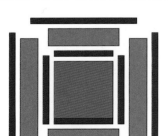

Making up

Sew the block, using the diagram as a guide, working outward from the center. Take care to keep accurate ¼in (6mm) seam allowances.

3 Plain Quilt 3

[Size]
5in (12.7cm)

CUTTING LIST

A   One 2½in (6.4cm) square
B   Two 2½ × ¾in (6.4 x 1.9cm) strips
B   Two 3 × ¾in (7.6 x 1.9cm) strips
B   Two 5 × ¾in (12.7 x 1.9cm) strips
B   Two 5½ × ¾in (14 x 1.9cm) strips
C   Two 3 × 1½in (7.6 x 3.8cm) strips
C   Two 5 × 1½in (12.7 x 3.8cm) strips

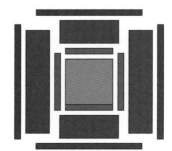

Making up

Sew the block, using the diagram as a guide, working outward from the center. Take care to keep accurate ¼in (6mm) seam allowances.

4 Plain Quilt 4

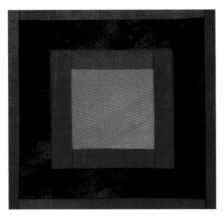

[Size]
5in (12.7cm)

CUTTING LIST

A One 2½in (6.4cm) square
B Two 2½ × 1in (6.4 x 2.5cm) strips
B Two 3½ × 1in (8.9 x 2.5cm) strips
B Two 5 × ¾in (12.7 x 1.9cm) strips
B Two 5½ × ¾in (14 x 1.9cm) strips
C Two 3½ × 1¼in (8.9 x 3.2cm) strips
C Two 5 × 1¼in (12.7 x 3.2cm) strips

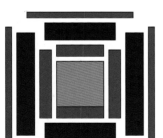

Making up

Sew the block, using the diagram as a guide, working outward from the center. Take care to keep accurate ¼in (6mm) seam allowances.

5 Plain Quilt 5

[Size]
5in (12.7cm)

CUTTING LIST

A One 3in (7.6cm) square
A Four 1¼in (3.2cm) squares
B Two 3 × ¾in (7.6 x 1.9cm) strips
B Two 3½ × ¾in (8.9 x 1.9cm) strips
C Four 3½ × 1¼in (8.9 x 3.2cm) strips
D Two 5 × ¾in (12.7 x 1.9cm) strips
D Two 5½ × ¾in (14 x 1.9cm) strips

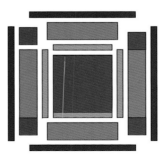

Making up

Sew the block, using the diagram as a guide, working outward from the center. Take care to keep accurate ¼in (6mm) seam allowances.

6 Framed Bars

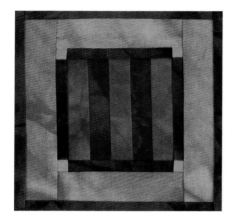

[Size]
5in (12.7cm)

CUTTING LIST

A
B
C
D
E

A   Three 3 × 1in (7.6 x 2.5cm) strips
B   Two 3 × 1in (7.6 x 2.5cm) strips
C   Four 3 × ¾in (7.6 x 1.9cm) strips
C   Two 5 × 1¼in (12.7 x 3.2cm) strips
C   Two 5½ × 1¼in (14 x 3.2cm) strips
D   Four ¾in (1.9cm) squares
E   Two 3½ × 1¼in (8.9 x 3.2cm) strips
E   Two 5 × 1¼in (12.7 x 3.2cm) strips

Making up

Sew the block, using the diagram as a guide, working outward from the center, sewing the five center strips together first. Take care to keep accurate ¼in (6mm) seam allowances.

Mix & Match
Quilt designs

Two different blocks can be combined in a checkerboard arrangement. The individual block edgings can be replaced with ½in- (1.3cm-) wide sashing. Blocks 10 and 12 were used above, and Blocks 2 and 6 below.

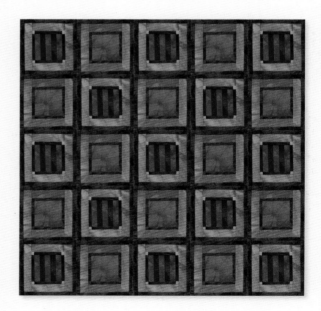

7 Diamond in the Square 1

[Size]
5in (12.7cm)

A

CUTTING LIST

A   One 2½in (6.4cm) square

B   Four 1½in (3.8cm) squares
B   Two 5 × ¾in (12.7 x 1.9cm) strips
B   Two 5½ × ¾in (14 x 1.9cm) strips

C   Two 2½ × 1in (6.4 x 2.5cm) strips
C   Two 3 × 1in (7.6 x 2.5cm) strips

D   Two 3 × 1¼in (7.6 x 3.2cm) strips
D   Two 5 × 1¼in (12.7 x 3.2cm) strips

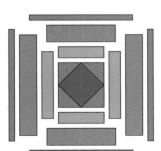

Making up

Sew the block, using the diagram as a guide, working outward from the center. Using the 2½in (6.4cm) square and four 1½in (3.8cm) squares, make the block center following the instructions for fast corners (see page 23). Take care to keep accurate ¼in (6mm) seam allowances.

8 Diamond in the Square 2

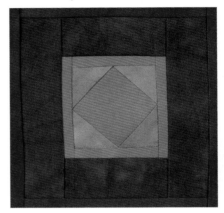

[Size]
5in (12.7cm)

CUTTING LIST

A   One 2½in (6.4cm) square
A   Two 2½ × ¾in (6.4 x 1.9cm) strips
A   Two 3 × ¾in (7.6 x 1.9cm) strips

B   Four 1½in (3.8cm) squares

C   Two 3 × 1½in (7.6 x 3.8cm) strips
C   Two 5 × 1½in (12.7 x 3.8cm) strips

D   Two 5 × ¾in (12.7 x 1.9cm) strips
D   Two 5½ × ¾in (14 x 1.9cm) strips

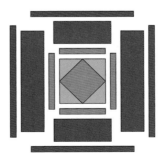

Making up

Sew the block, using the diagram as a guide, working outward from the center. Using the 2½in (6.4cm) square and four 1½in (3.8cm) squares, make the block center following the instructions for fast corners (see page 23). Take care to keep accurate ¼in (6mm) seam allowances.

9 Diamond in the Square 3

[Size]
5in (12.7cm)

CUTTING LIST

- A One 2½in (6.4cm) square
- B Four 1½in (3.8cm) squares
- C Four 2½ × 1in (6.4 x 2.5cm) strips
- C Two 5 × ¾in (12.7 x 1.9cm) strips
- C Two 5½ × ¾in (14 x 1.9cm) strips
- D Four 1in (2.5cm) squares
- E Four 3½ × 1¼in (8.9 x 3.2cm) strips
- F Four 1¼in (3.2cm) squares

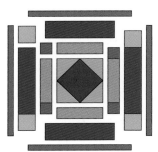

Making up

Sew the block, using the diagram as a guide, working outward from the center, sewing the five center strips together first. Take care to keep accurate ¼in (6mm) seam allowances.

10 Diamond in the Square 4

[Size]
5in (12.7cm)

CUTTING LIST

- A One 2in (5cm) square
- A Four 2½ × 1in (6.4 x 2.5cm) strips
- A Two 5 × ¾in (12.7 x 1.9cm) strips
- A Two 5½ × ¾in (14 x 1.9cm) strips
- B Eight 1¼in (3.2cm) squares
- B Four ¾in (1.9cm) squares
- B Four 1in (2.5cm) squares
- C Four 2 × ¾in (5 x 1.9cm) strips
- C Four 3½ × 1¼in (8.9 x 3.2cm) strips

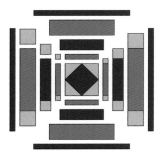

Making up

Sew the block, using the diagram as a guide, working outward from the center. Using the 2in (5cm) square and four of the 1¼in (3.2cm) squares, make the block center following the instructions for fast corners (see page 23). Take care to keep accurate ¼in (6mm) seam allowances.

11 Diamond in the Square 5

[Size]
5in (12.7cm)

CUTTING LIST

A   One 3in (7.6cm) square
A   Four 3 × ¾in (7.6 x 1.9cm) strips
B   Four 1¾in (4.4cm) squares
B   Four ¾in (1.9cm) squares
B   Four 1¼in (3.2cm) squares
C   Four 3½ × 1¼in (8.9 x 3.2cm) strips
D   Two 5 × ¾in (12.7 x 1.9cm) strips
D   Two 5½ × ¾in (14 x 1.9cm) strips

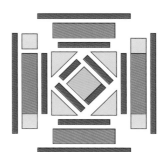

Making up

Sew the block, using the diagram as a guide, working outward from the center. Using the 3in (7.6cm) square and four 1¾in (4.4cm) squares, make the block center following the instructions for fast corners (see page 23). Take care to keep accurate ¼in (6mm) seam allowances.

12 Diamond in the Square 6

[Size]
5in (12.7cm)

CUTTING LIST

A   One 1¾in (4.4cm) square
B   Two 2½ × ¾in (6.4 x 1.9cm) strips
B   Two 1¾ × ¾in (4.4 x 1.9cm) strips
B   Two 3 × ¾in (7.6 x 1.9cm) strips
B   Two 3½ × ¾in (8.9 x 1.9cm) strips
B   Two 5 × ¾in (12.7 x 1.9cm)strips
B   Two 5 × ¾in (12.7 x 1.9cm) strips
C   Two 2⅛in (5.4cm) squares halved diagonally
C   Four 1¼in (3.2cm) squares
D   Four 3½ × 1¼in (8.9 x 3.2cm) strips

Making up

Sew the block, using the diagram as a guide, working outward from the center. Cut the two 2⅛in (5.4cm) squares in half diagonally and sew to the center unit. Take care to keep accurate ¼in (6mm) seam allowances.

13 Diamond in the Square 7

[Size]
5in (12.7cm)

CUTTING LIST

A One 2½in (6.4cm) square
A Eight ¾in (1.9cm) squares
B Four 1¾ × ¾in (4.4 x 1.9cm) strips
B Four 3 × ¾in (7.6 x 1.9cm) strips
B Two 5 × ¾in (12.7 x 1.9cm) strips
B Two 5½ × ¾in (14 x 1.9cm) strips
C Two 2⅛in (5.4cm) squares halved diagonally
C Four 1¼in (3.2cm) squares
D Four 3½ × 1¼in (8.9 x 3.2cm) strips

Making up

Sew the block, using the diagram as a guide, working outward from the center. Sew the shortest borders to the 2½in (6.4cm) square, then sew the corner triangles. Take care to keep accurate ¼in (6mm) seam allowances.

Mix & Match
Quilt designs

Twelve blocks make an interesting sampler quilt, ideal for a doll's bed or as a little wall hanging. Experiment to balance the blocks or make all the blocks from the same fabric selection for a more coordinated look. Here, Blocks 7, 12, and 2 make up the top row; 3, 5, and 8 the second row; 11, 9, and 4 the third row; and 6, 10, and 13 the bottom row.

Nine blocks make a cushion panel 15in (38cm) square. Add a border for a slightly larger cushion. The blocks used to make this panel are 4, 8, and 11.

Retro Revival

Mid-twentieth century design has experienced a big revival recently and there are many quilt fabric ranges in this style. So if funky and modern is your thing, try showing off the fabrics with this retro block selection. The finished blocks are all 5in (12.7cm) square. A pack of 10in (25.4cm) squares provides ample fabric for using in more than one block. Simple blocks like Four Patch allow you to show off the larger prints. Traditional blocks like Drunkard's Path and Robbing Peter to Pay Paul look great with retro prints, and the appliqué versions included here are easier than the original curved piecing. Or get groovy with Op Art designs.

14 Four Patch

[Size]
5in (12.7cm)

A

B

C

D

CUTTING LIST

A One 3in (7.6cm) square
B One 3in (7.6cm) square
C One 3in (7.6cm) square
D One 3in (7.6cm) square

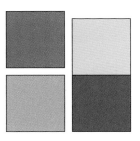

Making up

Sew the block, using the diagram as a guide. Sew pieces together in pairs and assemble as shown.

15 Houndstooth

[Size]
5in (12.7cm)

CUTTING LIST

A
B

A Four pieces from template 6 (page 119)
B Four pieces from template 6 (page 119)

Making up

Pieces can be cut from a 3in (7.6cm) strip. Sew the block, using the diagram as a guide. Sew pieces together in pairs and assemble as the Four Patch block (see page 44).

16 Whirligig

[Size]
5in (12.7cm)

CUTTING LIST

A
B

A Four pieces from template 6 (page 119)
B Four pieces from template 6 (page 119)

Making up

The units are the same as in the previous block, arranged differently. Pieces can be cut from a 3in (7.6cm) strip. Sew the block, using the diagram as a guide. Sew pieces together in pairs and assemble as the Four Patch block (see page 44).

17 Snail Trail

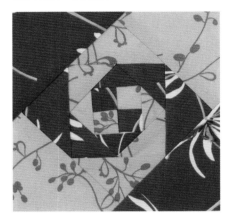

[Size]
5in (12.7cm)

CUTTING LIST

A

B

A Two 1⅛in (2.9cm) squares
A One 1¾in (4.4cm) square
A One 2⅛in (5.4cm) square
A One 2⅝in (6.7cm) square
A One 3⅜in (8.6cm) square

Repeat in fabric B

18 Festival Stars

[Size]
5in (12.7cm)

CUTTING LIST

A

B

C

A Two 3in (7.6cm) squares
B Two 3in (7.6cm) squares
C Four 3 × 1½in (7.6 × 3.8cm) strips

Making up

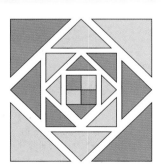

Cut all squares in half diagonally, except the 1⅛in (2.9cm) squares. Sew the block, using the diagram as a guide. Assemble the block from the center outward, starting with a tiny Four Patch in the center (see page 44). Sew pairs of triangles on either side of the block.

Making up

Sew one strip to each square, right sides together, stitching ¼in (6mm) from the edge of the strip and angling the strip so the top edge is

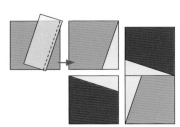

¾in (1.9cm) from the top left corner of the square and the bottom edge is ¼in (6mm) from the bottom left corner. Flip the strip over and press. Turn the square over and trim the strip to match the edge of the square before trimming away the edge of the square to match the ¼in (6mm) strip seam allowance. Make another four patches this way. Assemble as the Four Patch block (see page 44).

19 Wedge

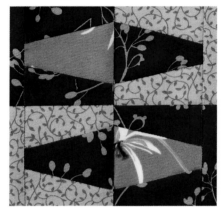

[Size]
5in (12.7cm)

CUTTING LIST

A

A Two 3 × 1in (7.6 × 2.5cm) strips
A Two pieces from template 3 (page 118)
A Two pieces from template 4 (page 118)
A Two pieces from template 4 (page 118), flipped for mirror image
B Two 3 × 1in (7.6 × 2.5cm) strips
B Two pieces from template 4 (page 118)
B Two pieces from template 4 (page 118), flipped for mirror image
C Two pieces from template 3 (page 118)

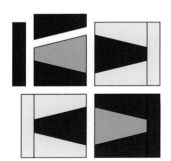

Making up
Sew the block, using the diagram as a guide. Assemble as the Four Patch block (see page 44).

20 Drunkard's Path

[Size]
5in (12.7cm)

CUTTING LIST

A

A Two 3in (7.6cm) squares
A Two pieces from template 12 (page 120)
B Two 3in (7.6cm) squares
B Two pieces from template 12 (page 120)

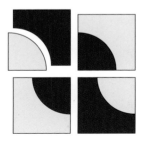

Making up
Sew the block, using the diagram a guide. The block is assembled as a Four Patch (see page 44). Sew pieces together in pairs, cutting the circle segments from the template and appliquéing one piece to each square. See page 25 for fused appliqué instructions. Stitch along the appliqué edges with a decorative stitch.

21 Robbing Peter to Pay Paul

[Size]
5in (12.7cm)

A ▪

B ▪

CUTTING LIST

A   One 5½in (14cm) square
B   Four segments from arc template 7 (page 119)

For reverse color block:
A   One 5½in (14cm) square
B   One center cross from template 7 (page 119)

22 Square and Dot

[Size]
5in (12.7cm)

A ▪

B ▪

CUTTING LIST

A   One 5½in (14cm) square
B   One rounded square from template 11 (page 120)

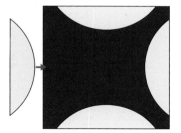

Making up

Make the block in pairs, cutting the segments from the edges of a 5½in (14cm) square. Use the segments to make one block and the remaining diagonal cross to make another. See page 25 for fused appliqué instructions. Make the block, using the diagram as a guide. Stitch along the appliqué edges with a decorative stitch.

Making up

Make the block, using the diagram as a guide. See page 25 for fused appliqué instructions. Stitch along the appliqué edges with a decorative stitch. For a three-color version, appliqué a circle onto the appliqué rounded square instead of cutting out the center.

23 Winding Ways

[Size]
5in (12.7cm)

CUTTING LIST

A   One 5½in (14cm) square
B   Four pieces from template 5 (page 118)

Mix & Match
Quilt designs

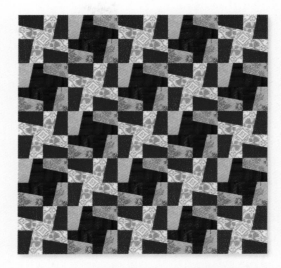

Alternate between two twisting blocks for a contemporary art panel. Blocks 15 and 16 have been used in this example.

Any block that is assembled in two halves can be split easily for an interesting effect. Block 25 (Pythagoras) can be set out in this way for a lively stepped diagonal with Block 18 (Festival Stars) completing the top right corner in the example left.

Making up
Make the block, using the diagram as a guide. Creasing a vertical and a diagonal line on the square helps you line up the pieces. See page 25 for fused appliqué instructions. Stitch along the appliqué edges with a decorative stitch.

24 Retro Bird

[Size]
5in (12.7cm)

CUTTING LIST

A One 5½in (14cm) square
B One piece from template 1 (page 118)
C One piece from template 2 (page 118)

Making up

Make the block, using the diagram as a guide. See page 25 for fused appliqué instructions. Stitch along the appliqué edges with a decorative stitch. Stitch the bird's legs with machine straight stitch. Stitch an eye or appliqué a button.

25 Pythagoras

[Size]
5in (12.7cm)

CUTTING LIST

A One piece from template 10 (page 120)
A One piece from template 10 (page 120), flipped for mirror image
A Two pieces from template 8 (page 120)
B One piece from template 9 (page 120)
C Two pieces from template 8 (page 120)
C Two pieces from template 8 (page 120), flipped for mirror image
D Two pieces from template 8 (page 120) flipped for mirror image

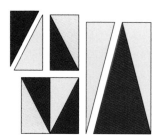

Making up

Sew the block, using the diagram as a guide. Sew triangles together to make rectangles, then assemble to make the block.

Strippy

[Size]
5in (12.7cm)

CUTTING LIST

A One 5½in × 1½in (14cm × 2.5cm) strip
B One 5½in × 1½in (14cm × 2.5cm) strip
C One 5½in × 1½in (14cm × 2.5cm) strip
D One 5½in × 1½in (14cm × 2.5cm) strip
E One 5½in × 1½in (14cm × 2.5cm) strip

A

B

C

D

E

PROJECT: MINI TOTE BAG

Combine three blocks—Blocks 19, 21 (with an extra appliqué dot), and 25 were used here—with some additional pieces of fabric to make an easy tote bag, following the basic bag instructions on page 31. By using one block that is made in two parts, each side of the bag uses one and a half blocks. Join these side panels with a strip of fabric across the bag base and add another strip to each end of your bag panel before quilting (see quilting, page 28). The finished bag panel is used as a pattern for the lining, so it is easy to make the lining the right size. Webbing makes a quick and easy pair of handles, sewn between the lining and the outside of the bag. It's the perfect size for your lunchtime shopping!

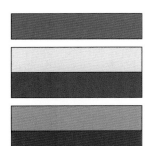

Making up

Sew the block, using the diagram as a guide. Arrange the strips, alternating between light and dark fabrics. Vary the strips in adjacent blocks for a strippy border or use up scraps left over from the other blocks.

Thrifty Thirties

Thirties-style reproduction fabrics are fresh and pretty and full of vintage charm, using printed patterns inspired by the old feedsack fabrics—printed animal feed sacks—that thrifty housewives used to recycle into patchwork and appliqué. Popular designs and images of that era make delightful little blocks, whether you are planning a special old-fashioned teatime, celebrating Art Deco architecture, or enjoying the glamour of travel with the Airplane block. A strip roll and matching charm pack of reproduction thirties' fabrics provides the long pieces and squares needed for these blocks. Choose a background fabric to set off your thirties' fabrics, like the pastel lemon weave here, and have fun—the sky's the limit! Finished blocks are 5in (12.7cm).

27 Sunburst

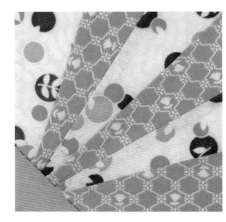

[Size]
5in (12.7cm)

CUTTING LIST

A
B
C

A	One piece from templates 19 and 21 (page 122)
A	One piece from template 20 (page 122), flipped
B	One piece from templates 19 and 21 (page 122), flipped
B	One piece from template 20 (page 122)
C	One 2⅜in (6cm) square, halved diagonally

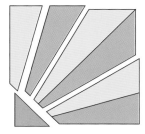

Making up

Sew the block, using the diagram as a guide. Sew the pieces together in pairs. Sew the triangle corner last. Take care not to stretch the bias edges as you sew. Keep the leftover C triangle for the next block or make blocks in pairs.

28 Art Deco

[Size]
5in (12.7cm)

A
B
C
D
E

CUTTING LIST

A One piece from template 19 (page 122)
B One piece from template 20 (page 122)
C One piece from template 16 (page 121)
C One piece from template 18 (page 121)
D One piece from template 17 (page 121)

Cut all the above again using the templates flipped

E One 2⅜in (6cm) square, halved diagonally

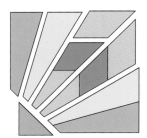

Making up

Sew the block, using the diagram as a guide. Sew the sunray pieces together in pairs. Sew the triangle corner last. Take care not to stretch the bias edges as you sew. Keep the leftover C triangle for another block or make blocks in pairs.

29 Art Deco Steps

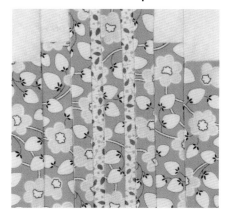

[Size]
5in (12.7cm)

A
B
C

CUTTING LIST

A Two 4¼ × 1¼in (10.8 × 3.2cm) strips
A Two 4¾ × 1¼in (12 × 3.2cm) strips
A Three 5½ × 1½in (14 × 3.8cm) strips
B Two 5½ × ¾in (14 × 1.9cm) strips
C Two 1¼in (3.2cm) squares
C Two 1¾ × 1¼in (4.4 × 3.2cm) strips

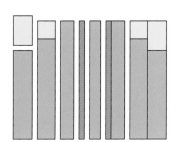

Making up

Sew the block, using the diagram as a guide. Sew the pieces together into strips and sew the strips together in pairs to make the block. Press the narrow B strips toward the C fabric, to reduce bulk.

30 Chinese Coins

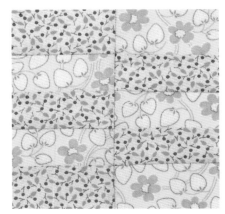

[Size]
5in (12.7cm)

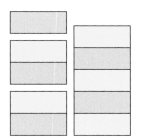

A

B

CUTTING LIST

A   Five 1½ × 3in strips (3.8 × 7.6cm)

B   Five 1½ × 3in strips (3.8 × 7.6cm)

Making up
Sew the block, using the diagram as a guide. Sew the pieces together to make strips and sew the strips together to complete the block.

31 Parquet

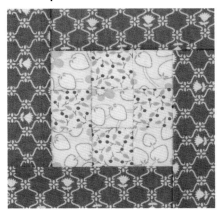

[Size]
5in (12.7cm)

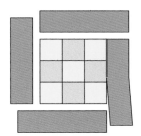

A

B

C

CUTTING LIST

A   Five 1½in (3.8cm) squares

B   Four 1½in (3.8cm) squares

C   Four 1½ × 4½in (3.8 × 11.4cm) strips

Making up
Sew the block, using the diagram as a guide. The center is a Nine Patch (see page 68). Sew the block from the center outward. Sew only 1½in (3.8cm) of the first seam, as highlighted in red. Press all seams toward edge of block. Sew the next strip across the top of the block, then sew the other two strips in sequence. Finish by completing the first seam, overlapping the stitching line by about ½in (1.3cm).

32 Flying Geese

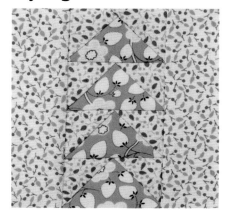

[Size]
5in (12.7cm)

CUTTING LIST

A   Two 5½ × 1¾in (14 × 4.4cm) strips
B   Four 3 × 1¾in (7.6 × 4.4cm) strips
C   Eight 1¾in (4.4cm) squares

Making up

Sew the block, using the diagram as a guide. Using the B and C pieces, make four Flying Geese units. Assemble the block in strips.

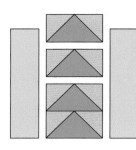

Mix & Match
Quilt designs

Tea for two? Enjoy afternoon tea thirties-style by making up the center of this design with four of Block 35, surrounded by Blocks 33, 34, and 36. Have fun decorating the cakes with different button embellishments.

Celebrate Art Deco architectural designs with Blocks 27, 28, and 29, arranging the blocks to echo the sunburst center.

33 Teacup

[Size]
5in (12.7cm)

CUTTING LIST

A   A   Two 5½ × 1½in (14 × 3.8cm) strips
B   A   Two 2in (5cm) squares
       A   One piece from template 14 (page 121)
C   A   One piece from template 14 (page 121), flipped
       B   One piece from template 13 (page 121)
D   C   One 5½ × 1in (14 × 2.5cm) strip
       D   One piece from template 15 (page 121)

Making up

Sew the block, using the diagram as a guide. Appliqué the D piece using the fused appliqué method (see page 25). Take care not to stretch the bias edges when sewing the teacup to the background pieces. Sew the C strip to one of the 5½ × 1½in (14 × 3.8cm) strips. Add the triangle corners using the 2in (5cm squares) and the fast corners method (see page 23).

34 Tea Plate

[Size]
5in (12.7cm)

CUTTING LIST

A   A   One 4½in (11.4cm) square
B   B   Four 4½ × 1in (11.4 × 2.5cm) strips
       C   Four 2in (5cm) squares
C   D   One 3in (7.6cm) diameter circle
D

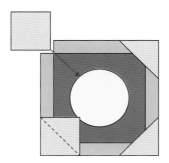

Making up

Sew the block, using the diagram as a guide. Appliqué the D piece using the fused appliqué method (see page 25). Sew the four 4½ × 1in (11.4 × 2.5cm) strips to the square; they will not meet at the corners, but this will not be seen. Using the 2in (5cm) squares, add the corner triangles, using the fast corners method (see page 23).

35 Dresden Plate Fan

[Size]
5in (12.7cm)

CUTTING LIST

A
B
C
D
E

- A   One 5½in (14cm) square
- B   One piece from template 24 (page 123)
- C   One piece from template 24 (page 123)
- D   One piece from template 24 (page 123)
- E   One piece from template 24 (page 123)

36 Cupcake

[Size]
5in (12.7cm)

CUTTING LIST

A
B
C

- A   One 5½in (14cm) square
- B   One piece from template 22 (page 122)
- B   One piece from template 23 (page 122)

Making up

Sew the block, using the diagram as a guide. To make the pointed segments, fold one piece in half lengthwise, right sides together, and sew a ¼in (6mm) seam across the wide end. Turn this end right side out to make a point and press. Make four segments in this way. Sew segments together in pairs and sew pairs of segments together. Hand-appliqué the shape to the background square (see hand appliqué, page 25). Four of these blocks will make one whole Dresden Plate.

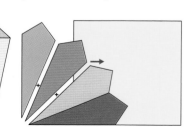

Making up

Make the block, using the diagram as a guide. See page 25 for fused appliqué instructions. Stitch along the appliqué edges with a decorative stitch. Embellish the top of your cupcake with a button or beads to suggest iced details.

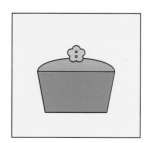

37 Modernist Twist

[Size]
5in (12.7cm)

CUTTING LIST

A
B

A One 5¼in (13.3cm) square, quartered diagonally
B Four pieces from template 25 (page 123)

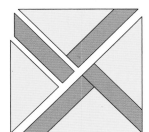

Making up
Sew the block, using the diagram as a guide. Sew each B strip to each triangle, taking care not to stretch the bias edges.

38 Propeller

[Size]
5in (12.7cm)

CUTTING LIST

A
B

A Two 2⅞in (7.3cm) squares
A Five 1½in (3.8cm) squares
B Two 2⅞in (7.3cm) squares
B Four 1½in (3.8cm) squares

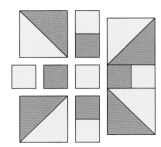

Making up
Sew the block, using the diagram as a guide. Using the larger squares, make four triangle squares (see page 19). Sew pairs of smaller A and B squares. Assemble the block in rows.

39 Airplane

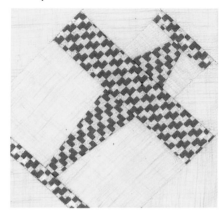

[Size]
5in (12.7cm)

CUTTING LIST

A

B

A   One 2⅝in (7.75cm) square, halved diagonally
A   One 2⅛in (6.5cm) square, halved diagonally
A   One 3¼in (10.5cm) square, quartered diagonally
A   One piece from template 29 (page 123)
A   One piece from template 29 (page 123), flipped
A   One piece from template 26 (page 123)
A   One piece from template 26 (page 123), flipped
B   One 2¼in × ⅞in (6cm × 2.5cm) strip
B   One 5⅛in × 1½in (13cm × 4cm) strip
B   One piece from template 30 (page 123)
B   One piece from template 27 (page 123)
B   One piece from template 28 (page 123)

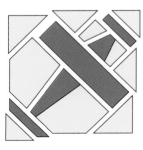

Making up

Keep two of the 3¼in (10.5cm) quartered triangles for another block. Sew the block, using the diagram as a guide. Sew one piece 26 to either side of piece 27 and one piece 29 to either side of piece 30. Sew piece 28 to one of the smaller half-square triangles. Sew the tail section and wing to the airplane body and sew the larger half-square triangles to each side. Sew the propeller to the front of the airplane, sew one quarter-square triangle to each end and the remaining smaller half square triangle to the front of the propeller. Sew the two halves of the block together.

Mix & Match

Quilt designs

Block 39 looks effective with the planes flying in formation in between diagonal rows of Block 35, rotated alternately. Make the airplanes from the same fabrics for your own airline livery.

Stay airborne with more aerobatics, combining Block 39 with Blocks 37 and 38, with the planes weaving in and out of each other's flight paths.

Stars and Pinwheels

This selection of twinkling stars and twirling pinwheels includes many of our quilting heritage favorites. Pinwheel (Block 40) is the easiest to make but, as all these blocks are made from various squares, triangle squares (see page 19), and Flying Geese units (see page 55), none is particularly challenging. A pack of 10in (25.4cm) squares in faded primary colors provides plenty of blues and yellows for a heavenly color scheme, with occasional accents in red. This larger square size also gives ample fabric for several blocks to share the same fabrics. As most of the blocks require only three different fabrics at most, they are also ideal for Americana themes. The blocks are just 3in (7.6cm) at finished size; however, Blocks 50 and 51 are larger, at 4in (10.2cm) square.

Pinwheel

[Size]
3in (7.6cm)

A

B

CUTTING LIST
A   Two 2⅜in (6cm) squares
B   Two 2⅜in (6cm) squares

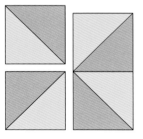

Making up

Sew the block, using the diagram as a guide. Make the four triangle squares following the instructions on page 19. Assemble the block as a Four Patch (see page 44).

41 Turnstile

[Size]
3in (7.6cm)

CUTTING LIST

A

B

A One 2¾in (7cm) square, quartered diagonally

B One 2¾in (7cm) square, quartered diagonally

B Two 2⅜in (6cm) squares, halved diagonally

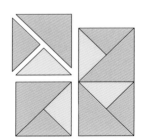

Making up
Sew the block, using the diagram as a guide. Sew the smaller triangles together in pairs and sew to the larger triangles. Take care not to stretch the bias edges. Assemble the block as a Four Patch (see page 44).

42 Broken Pinwheel

[Size]
3in (7.6cm)

CUTTING LIST

A

B

C

A One 2¾in (7cm) square, quartered diagonally

B One 2¾in (7cm) square, quartered diagonally

C Two 2⅜in (6cm) squares, halved diagonally

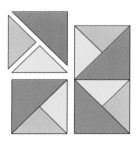

Making up
Sew the block, using the diagram as a guide. Sew the smaller triangles together in pairs and sew to the larger triangles. Take care not to stretch the bias edges. Assemble the block as a Four Patch (see page 44).

43 Eight-pointed Star

[Size]
3in (7.6cm)

CUTTING LIST

A

B

- A Eight 1¼in (3.2cm) squares
- A One 2in (5cm) square
- B Four 1¼ × 2in (3.2 × 5cm) strips
- B Four 1¼in (3.2cm) squares

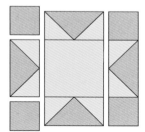

Making up

Sew the block, using the diagram as a guide. Using the four B strips and eight A squares, make four Flying Geese units (see page 55). Assemble the block in strips.

44 Morning Star

[Size]
3in (7.6cm)

CUTTING LIST

A

B

- A Eight 1¼in (3.2cm) squares
- B One 2in (5cm) square
- B Four 1¼ × 2in (3.2 × 5cm) strips
- B Four 1¼in (3.2cm) squares

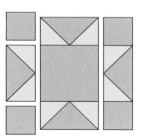

Making up

Sew the block, using the diagram as a guide. Using the four B strips and eight A squares, make four Flying Geese units (see page 55). Assemble the block in strips.

45 Autograph Star

[Size]
3in (7.6cm)

CUTTING LIST

A
B
C
C
D
D

A   One 1 × 2in (2.5 × 5cm) strip of plain fabric
B   Two 1 × 2in strip (2.5 × 5cm)
C   Eight 1¼in (3.2cm) squares
D   Four 1¼ × 2in (3.2 × 5cm) strips
D   Four 1¼in (3.2cm) squares

Making up

Sew the block, using the diagram as a guide. Using the four D strips and eight C squares; make four Flying Geese units (see page 55). Assemble the block in strips. The plain strip can be decorated with a name or inscription.

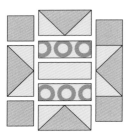

Mix & Match
Quilt designs

Blocks 40 and 49 form the swirling center of the nine-patch design above, with Block 41 as a border, calmed by the symmetrical Block 43 in the corners. Alternating Block 42 with Blocks 43 and 45 makes a lively design with space to write autographs or messages on the stars.

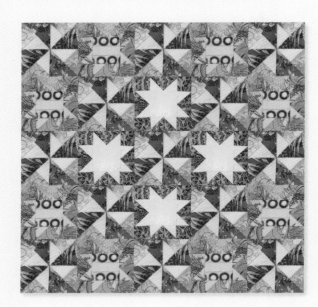

46

Friendship Star

[Size]
3in (7.6cm)

CUTTING LIST

A
B

A   Two 1⅞in (4.8cm) squares
A   One 1½in (3.8cm) square
B   Two 1⅞in (4.8cm) squares
B   Four 1½in (3.8cm) squares

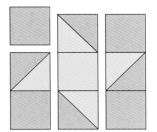

Making up
Sew the block, using the diagram as a guide. Using the 1⅞in (4.8cm) squares, make four triangle squares (see page 19). Assemble the block as a Nine Patch (see page 68).

47

Nine-patch Star

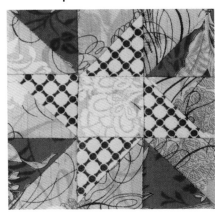

[Size]
3in (7.6cm)

CUTTING LIST

A
B
C

A   Two 1⅞in (4.8cm) squares
B   Four 1⅞in (4.8cm) squares
B   One 1½in (3.8cm) square
C   Two 1⅞in (4.8cm) squares

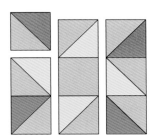

Making up
Sew the block, using the diagram as a guide. Using the 1⅞in (4.8cm) squares, make eight triangle squares (see page 19). Assemble the block as a Nine Patch (see page 68).

48 Suzannah

[Size]
3in (7.6cm)

CUTTING LIST

 A

 B

 C

A   Four 1¼ × 2in (3.2 × 5cm) strips
B   Four 1¼ × 2in (3.2 × 5cm) strips
C   Four 1¼in (3.2cm) squares

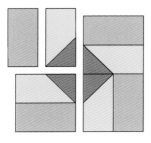

Making up

Sew the block, using the diagram as a guide. Use the four A strips and four C squares to make four units with triangles (see Flying Geese, page 55). Assemble the block as a Four Patch (see page 44).

Mix & Match
Quilt designs

In the example above, Block 50 appears to spin clockwise and Block 51 counter-clockwise, so combining the two as a checkerboard creates a fascinating secondary pattern. In the sampler on the left, all the blocks in this chapter have been used together, balanced across the patchwork.

49 Louisiana

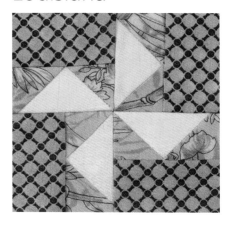

[Size]
3in (7.6cm)

A

B

C

CUTTING LIST

A Four 1¼ × 2in (3.2 × 5cm) strips
B Four 1¼ × 2in (3.2 × 5cm) strips
C Eight 1¼in (3.2cm) squares

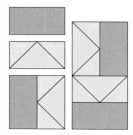

Making up

Sew the block, using the diagram as a guide. Using the four A strips and eight C squares, make Flying Geese units (see page 55). Assemble the block as a Four Patch (see page 44).

50 Seesaw

[Size]
4in (10.2cm)

A

B

B

CUTTING LIST

A Four 1¼ × 2in (3.2 × 5cm) strips
B Four 1¼ × 2in (3.2 × 5cm) strips
B Eight 1¼in (3.2cm) squares
C Four 1¼in (3.2cm) squares

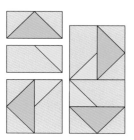

Making up

Sew the block, using the diagram as a guide. Use the four A strips and eight B squares to make Flying Geese units (see page 55). Use the remaining pieces and the same instructions to make the strips with triangles. Assemble the block as a Four Patch (see page 44).

Nextdoor Neighbor

[Size]
4in (10.2cm)

CUTTING LIST

A

B

C

A   Two 1¼ × 2in (3.2 × 5cm) strips
A   Two 1¼in (3.2cm) squares
B   Two 1¼ × 2in (3.2 × 5cm) strips
B   Two 1¼in (3.2cm) squares
C   Four 1¼ × 2in (3.2 × 5cm) strips
C   Eight 1¼in (3.2cm) squares

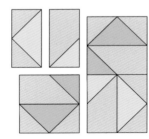

Making up

Sew the block, using the diagram as a guide. Using the four A and B strips and eight C squares, make Flying Geese units (see page 55). Use the remaining pieces and the same instructions to make the strips with triangles. Assemble the block as a Four Patch (see page 44).

PROJECT: BROOCHES

Using just one block per brooch, these are perfect projects for swaps or gifts. Before backing the brooches, give the stars and pinwheels some extra twinkle by machine-quilting each block in a simple design with metallic thread—just relax and doodle with the thread. Sew a charm to the bottom corner for a finishing touch.

YOU WILL NEED (FOR EACH BROOCH):

One 3in (7.6cm) block of your choice
One 3½in (8.9cm) piece of batting
One 3½in (8.9cm) piece of muslin
One 3½in (8.9cm) coordinating
    square for backing
One safety pin or brooch pin
Charm of your choice
Machine-quilting threads
    of your choice

1 Layer and quilt the block, batting, and muslin. Quilt a simple design, as desired.

2 Place the quilted block and backing fabric right sides together. Machine-sew all round, leaving a 2in (5cm) gap along one side. Trim away excess batting within the seam allowance. Clip the corners, turn the brooch right side out through the gap, and slip-stitch the gap closed.

3 Hand-sew a charm to the bottom corner and oversew the completed panel to the safety pin or brooch pin, which should be centered on the back.

English Traditions

These small and simple quilt blocks are found in many eighteenth-century English patchworks. Some are still known and made today, while others will be less familiar. English paper piecing (see page 21) was the most popular technique over 200 years ago, and is used here for Blocks 62 and 63. Other blocks are suitable for machine piecing. The original names of these blocks are now mysteries; some are known by nineteenth-century names, while others are anonymous. A pack of 10in (25.4cm) squares in antique-style prints, suitably pale-colored to look like faded old quilts, gives these blocks an old-time charm, with more than a hint of a cottage garden. Look out for similar collections including chintz-style prints: fabrics that were once the height of fashionable elegance. The finished blocks are 4½in (11.4cm) square.

52 Nine Patch 1

[Size]
4½in (11.4cm)

  A

  B

  C

CUTTING LIST

A   Four 2in (5cm) squares
B   Four 2in (5cm) squares
C   One 2in (5cm) square

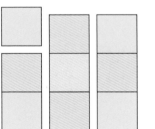

Making up
Sew the block, using the diagram as a guide. Sew the squares into strips, then sew the strips together to complete the block.

53 Nine Patch 2

[Size]
4½in (11.4cm)

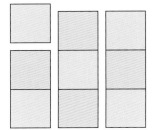

A
B

CUTTING LIST

A   Five 2in (5cm) squares
B   Four 2in (5cm) squares

Making up

Sew the block, using the diagram as a guide. Sew the squares into strips, then sew the strips together to complete the block.

54 Shoofly

[Size]
4½in (11.4cm)

A
B
C

CUTTING LIST

A   Four 2in (5cm) squares
A   Two 2⅜in (6cm) squares
B   One 2in (5cm) square
C   Two 2⅜in (6cm) squares

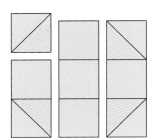

Making up

Sew the block, using the diagram as a guide. Using the 2⅜in (6cm) squares, make triangle squares (see page 19). Sew the squares into strips, then sew the strips together to complete the block.

55 Broken Dishes

[Size]
4½in (11.4cm)

A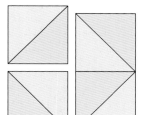

CUTTING LIST

A   Two 3⅛in (7.9cm) squares
B   Two 3⅛in (7.9cm) squares

Making up
Sew the block, using the diagram as a guide. Make triangle squares (see page 19). Sew the triangle squares into strips, then sew the strips together to complete the block.

56 Triangle Squares

[Size]
4½in (11.4cm)

A
B
C
D
E
F

CUTTING LIST

A   Four 2⅜in (6cm) squares
B   Two 2⅜in (6cm) squares
C   One 2⅜in (6cm) square
D   One 2⅜in (6cm) square
E   One 2⅜in (6cm) square
F   One 2⅜in (6cm) square

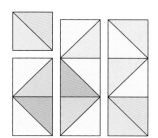

Making up
Sew the block, using the diagram as a guide. Make triangle squares (see page 19)—four A and B; two of A and C, A and D, E and F. Sew the triangle squares into strips, then sew the strips together to complete the block. One A and B triangle square will be left over for another block.

57 Triangle Square on Point

[Size]
4½in (11.4cm)

CUTTING LIST

A   One 4¹/₁₆in (10.3cm) square for triangle square
B   One 4¹/₁₆in (10.3cm) square for triangle square
C   Four 3⅛in (7.9cm) squares, halved diagonally

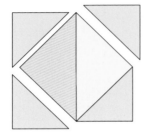

Making up

Sew the block, using the diagram as a guide. Using the A and B squares, make two triangle squares (see page 19). Keep one for another block. Sew the corner triangles, adding opposite corners in pairs.

Mix & Match
Quilt designs

Medallion arrangements were popular for eighteenth-century quilts, often with larger patches used in the outer borders and more detailed designs used at the center. Blocks 57, 58, and 59 are bordered with Blocks 63 and 64 in the sample above. Below, Blocks 53 and 64 are used for a Nine-Patch center, with a double border of Blocks 55 and 62.

58 Four Patch on Point

[Size]
4½in (11.4cm)

CUTTING LIST

A   Two 2⅛in (5.4cm) squares
B   Two 2⅛in (5.4cm) squares
C   Two 3⅛in (7.9cm) squares, halved diagonally

Making up

Sew the block, using the diagram as a guide. Using the A and B squares, make a Four Patch (see page 44). Sew the corner triangles, adding opposite corners in pairs.

59 Nine Patch on Point

[Size]
4½in (11.4cm)

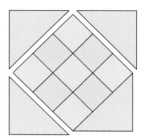

CUTTING LIST

A   Five 1⁹⁄₁₆in (4cm) squares
B   Four 1⁹⁄₁₆in (4cm) squares
C   Two 3⅛in (7.9cm) squares, halved diagonally

Making up

Sew the block, using the diagram as a guide. Using the A and B squares, make a Nine Patch 1 (see page 68). Sew the corner triangles, adding opposite corners in pairs.

60 Squares on Point

[Size]
4½in (11.4cm)

CUTTING LIST

A

B

C

A Four 2¹⁄₁₆in (5.2cm) squares
B One 2¹⁄₁₆in (5.2cm) square
C Two 2in (5cm) squares, halved diagonally
C One 3½in (8.9cm) square, quartered diagonally

Sew the block, using the diagram as a guide. Sew squares into strips and sew strips together to complete the block, adding corner triangles last.

61 Kaleidoscope

[Size]
4½in (11.4cm)

CUTTING LIST

A
B
C

A Four pieces from template 31 (page 124)
B Four pieces from template 31 (page 124)
C Two 2⁹⁄₁₆in (6.5cm) squares, halved diagonally

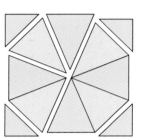

Making up

Sew the block, using the diagram as a guide. Assemble the block center pieces into quarters, as shown, and sew the block together in two halves. Add the corner triangles last.

62 Hexagon Rosette

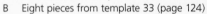

[Size]
4½in (11.4cm)

A
B
C

CUTTING LIST

A One 5in (12.7cm) square
B Six pieces from template 32 (page 124)
C One piece from template 32 (page 124)

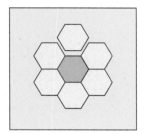

Making up

Sew the block, using the diagram as a guide. Hand-sew the hexagon rosette, following the instructions for English paper piecing (see page 21) and centering a fabric motif on each hexagon if possible. Sew each hexagon to the central hexagon, then join the other edges. Appliqué the hexagon to the center of the square.

63 Octagon Rosette

[Size]
4½in (11.4cm)

A
B

CUTTING LIST

A   One 5in (12.7cm) square
B   Eight pieces from template 33 (page 124)

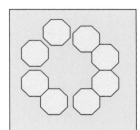

Making up

Sew the block, using the diagram as a guide. Hand-sew the octagon rosette, following the instructions for English paper piecing (see page 21) and centering a fabric motif on each hexagon if possible. Sew octagons together in pairs and join to make a ring. Appliqué the hexagon to the center of the square.

64 Plume

[Size]
4½in (11.4cm)

CUTTING LIST

A   One 5in (12.7cm) square
B   One piece from template 34 (page 124)
C   One piece from template 35 (page 124)
C   One piece from template 35 (page 124), flipped
D   One piece from template 36 (page 124)
D   One piece from template 36 (page 124), flipped

A
B
C
D

Making up

See page 25 for fused appliqué instructions. Make the block, using the diagram as a guide. Slightly overlap template 35 pieces with the central and edge pieces when fusing the appliqué. Stitch along the appliqué edges with a decorative stitch.

Mix & Match

Quilt designs

Eighteenth-century quilters seem to have collected blocks for a kind of album patchwork, repeating the blocks in a symmetrical layout—the one above uses all the blocks in this chapter. Nine different blocks (left) would make a pretty coordinating pillowslip.

Crazy Colors

Modern art quilters make extensive use of irregular piecing. Random cuts are sliced through stacks of squares so there are multiple pieces of the same wedge shapes. These are rearranged for the block, so multiple blocks are made from one set of cuts. Alternatively narrow strips can be sewn to a foundation (see Crazy Patchwork and Appliqué, page 24). A 6in (15.2cm) charm pack is ideal for these blocks, as most start with a stack of squares. Batik and marbled salt dyes enhance the art quilt style but modern painterly prints would be equally suitable. Try silks or reproduction prints if you want a Victorian crazy patchwork look. The piecing techniques mean all the blocks finish with uneven edges and are trimmed to 4½in (11.4cm) square; the finished blocks measure 4in (10.2cm).

65 Random Slice

[Size]
4in (10.2cm)

A
B

CUTTING LIST
A One 6in (15.2cm) square
B One 6in (15.2cm) square

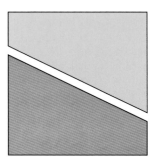

Making up

Make blocks in pairs. Stack the two squares and slice through at an angle, as shown. Take the top piece from the uppermost fabric and the bottom piece from the lower fabric. Sew the block, using the diagram as a guide—there is no need to line up the outer edges exactly. Trim the finished blocks to 4½in (11.4cm) square (see Crazy Patchwork and Appliqué, page 24).

66 Slice with Strip

[Size]
4in (10.2cm)

A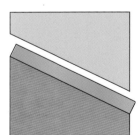
B
C

CUTTING LIST

A One 6in (15.2cm) square
B One 6in (15.2cm) square
C Two 6 × 1in (15.2 × 2.5cm) strips

Making up

Make blocks in pairs. Stack and cut the squares as for the previous block. Sew the block, using the diagram as a guide, inserting the strip between the two patchwork pieces. The strip will seem short for the block, but the finished blocks are trimmed to 4½in (11.4cm) square (see Crazy Patchwork and Appliqué, page 24).

67 Crisscross

[Size]
4in (10.2cm)

A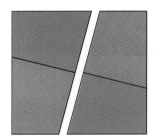
B

CUTTING LIST

A One 6in (15.2cm) square
B One 6in (15.2cm) square

Making up

Make blocks in pairs. Stack, cut, and make two blocks (see Block 66). Layer the blocks, both right sides up, and cut across again. Taking one piece from the upper layer and one from the lower layer, complete the block, lining up the seams at the block center (the edges will be uneven). Trim the blocks to 4½in (11.4cm) square (see Crazy Patchwork and Appliqué, page 24).

68 Crisscross Strips

[Size]
4in (10.2cm)

CUTTING LIST

A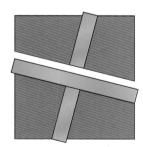

B

A   One 6in (15.2cm) square
B   Two 6 × 1in (15.2 cm × 2.5cm) strips

Making up

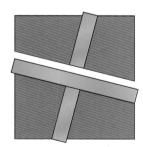

Make blocks individually. Cut the square diagonally and sew with one of the strips (see Block 66). Cut across the patchwork and insert the second strip between the two patchwork pieces, lining up the first strip across this seam. The strip will seem short for the block, but the finished block is trimmed to 4½in (11.4cm) square (see Crazy Patchwork and Appliqué, page 24).

69 Delectable Mountains (random cut)

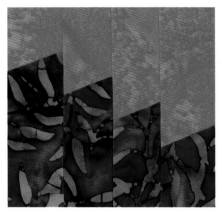

[Size]
4in (10.2cm)

CUTTING LIST

A

B

A   One 6in (15.2cm) square
B   One 6in (15.2cm) square

Making up

SWAP STRIPS

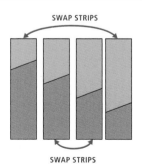

SWAP STRIPS

Make blocks in pairs. Make two blocks (see Block 65), lining up the edges of the block. Cut the block into four 1½in (3.8cm) strips, across the diagonal seam. Rearrange the pieces as shown and sew together. Repeat with the second block. Trim the finished blocks to 4½in (11.4cm) square (see Crazy Patchwork and Appliqué, page 24).

70 Layered Wedges

[Size]
4in (10.2cm)

CUTTING LIST

A One 6in (15.2cm) square
B One 6in (15.2cm) square
C One 6in (15.2cm) square

A

B

C

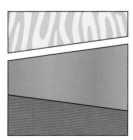

Making up

Make blocks in threes. Stack the three squares and slice through twice at an angle, as shown. Sew the block, using the diagram as a guide, using one piece of each fabric—there is no need to line up the outer edges exactly. Trim the finished blocks to 4½in (11.4cm) square (see Crazy Patchwork and Appliqué, page 24).

Mix & Match
Quilt designs

Many of these blocks are made in pairs, trios, or larger sets, which lend themselves to exciting abstract designs—Block 73 bordered with Blocks 76 and 77 above, and multiple sets of Blocks 74 and 75 below.

71 Stripes and Wedges

[Size]
4in (10.2cm)

CUTTING LIST

A
B
C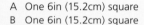
D

A One 6in (15.2cm) square
B One 6in (15.2cm) square
C One 6in (15.2cm) square
D Six 6 × 1in (15.2 × 2.5cm) strips

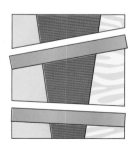

Making up
Make blocks in threes, as for Block 70. Cut across the patchwork twice and insert the strip between the patchwork pieces, as shown. Each block can be cut separately for more variety. The strip will seem short for the block, but the finished block is trimmed to 4½in (11.4cm) square (see Crazy Patchwork and Appliqué, page 24).

72 Clouds and Mountains

[Size]
4in (10.2cm)

CUTTING LIST

A
B
C

A One 6in (15.2cm) square
B One 6in (15.2cm) square
C One 6in (15.2cm) square

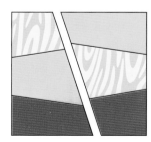

Making up
Make blocks in threes, as for Block 70. Layer all three blocks, right sides up, and cut across again. Taking two pieces from different layers, complete the block. Do not line up any seams at the center. One block will have the purple band through the middle. Trim the blocks to 4½in (11.4cm) square (see Crazy Patchwork and Appliqué, page 24).

73 Random Nine Patch

[Size]
4in (10.2cm)

CUTTING LIST

A
B
C

A One 6in (15.2cm) square
B One 6in (15.2cm) square
C One 6in (15.2cm) square

Making up

Make blocks in threes, as for Block 70. Layer all three blocks, right sides up, and cut across twice again. Taking three pieces from different layers, complete the block. Do not line up any seams at the center. Trim the blocks to 4½in (11.4cm) square (see Crazy Patchwork and Appliqué, page 24).

74 Random Square

[Size]
4in (10.2cm)

CUTTING LIST

A
B
C
D
E

A One 6in (15.2cm) square
B One 6in (15.2cm) square
C One 6in (15.2cm) square
D One 6in (15.2cm) square
E One 6in (15.2cm) square

Making up

Make blocks in fives. Stack the five squares. Cut the first strip at an angle off the left side, then the bottom, then the right, then the top. Sew the block, using one piece of each fabric. The first two pieces will more or less match up, but the others will be too long; sew from the widest end and trim the other, or the block will be too small. Trim to 4½in (11.4cm) square (see Crazy Patchwork and Appliqué, page 24).

75 Spinning Square

[Size]
4in (10.2cm)

		CUTTING LIST
A		A One 6in (15.2cm) square
B		B One 6in (15.2cm) square
		C One 6in (15.2cm) square
C		D One 6in (15.2cm) square
		E One 6in (15.2cm) square
D		F One 6in (15.2cm) square
E		
F		

Making up

Make blocks in sixes. Stack the six squares. Cut just off the horizontal; cut twice at 60 degrees to that line. Sew each block in two halves, using one piece of each fabric. Match the pieces at the center; the triangles will seem too short, but the finished blocks are trimmed to 4½in (11.4cm) square (see Crazy Patchwork and Appliqué, page 24).

76 Triangular Strips

[Size]
4in (10.2cm)

		CUTTING LIST
A		A One 4½in (11.4cm) square
B		B, C, D Strips of scrap fabric of various lengths and widths
C		
D		

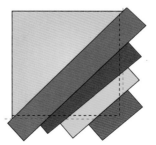

Making up

Make blocks individually. Mark a diagonal line across the square and a parallel line ¼in (6mm) away. Line up the longest strip against the second line and sew along the first line. Flip the strip over and press. Continue adding strips until half the square is covered. Turn the block over and machine-sew close to the strip edges, then trim the ends to match the square (see Crazy Patchwork and Appliqué, page 24).

77 Random Rosette

[Size]
4in (10.2cm)

CUTTING LIST

A One 4½in (11.4cm) plain square
B, C, D, E, F Strips of scrap fabric of
various lengths and widths

A
B
C
D
E
F

Making up

Make blocks individually. Pin a squarish piece to the center of the square. Machine-sew strips around it, flipping the strips over toward the outside of the block and pressing as you go. Continue adding strips at random angles until the square is covered. Turn the block over and machine-sew close to the edge, then trim strip ends to match the square (see Crazy Patchwork and Appliqué, page 24).

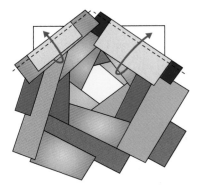

Mix & Match
Quilt designs

Rotating and mirroring blocks creates this abstract landscape above, with a horizontal strip arrangement, using Blocks 65, 67, 69, and 70. Blocks 65, 68, and 69 were also mirrored or rotated to give a sense of movement to this narrow wall hanging on the left.

Taupe Tranquillity

The restful neutral tones of taupe quilt fabrics originate in Japan, where these colors have been appreciated by quilters for several decades. Avoiding bright hues and using only those with a hint of gray gives traditional American blocks such as Cake Stand a new sophistication. Cute fabric prints featuring such motifs as little houses and sewing notions suggested fun new blocks like Dollhouse and Spool, while the Japanese Arrow Feathers block hints at the Japanese origins of the fabrics. Scraps left over from a larger quilting project show how easy taupes are to coordinate. Take care to maintain the taupe palette for a calm feeling, saving saturated colors for another project.

[Size]
5in (12.7cm)

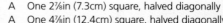

A
B
C
D

CUTTING LIST

A One 2⅞in (7.3cm) square, halved diagonally
A One 4⅞in (12.4cm) square, halved diagonally
A Two 3½ x 1½in (8.9 × 3.8cm) strips
B One 1⅞in (4.8cm) square, halved diagonally
C Two 1⅞in (4.8cm) squares, halved diagonally
C Two 1⅞in (4.8cm) squares, for triangle squares
D Three 1⅞in (4.8cm) squares, for triangle squares
E One 6in (15.2cm) piece of bias tape for handle

Making up

Use a 3in (7.6cm) circle template to draw the inner curve for the basket handle on the largest triangle; appliqué the bias tape (see fusible bias tape, page 25). Using the squares of fabric C and D, make the triangle squares and triangles. Sew the block, using the diagram as a guide. Add the 4⅞in (12.4cm) triangle last. Keep the two leftover large triangles for another block or make blocks in pairs.

79 Cake Stand

[Size]
5in (12.7cm)

CUTTING LIST

 A
 B
C

- A   One 2⅞in (7.3cm) square, halved diagonally
- A   One 3⅞in (9.8cm) square
- A   Two 3½ x 1½in (8.9 x 3.8cm) strips
- A   One 1½in (3.8cm) square
- A   Three 1⅞in (4.8cm) squares, for triangle squares
- B   One 3⅞in (9.8cm) square
- B   One 1⅞in (4.8cm) square, halved diagonally
- C   Three 1⅞in (4.8cm) squares, for triangle squares

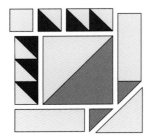

Making up

Sew the block, using the diagram as a guide. Using the 3⅞in (9.8cm) squares of fabric A and B, make the large triangle square first. Make the smaller triangle squares and add as borders. Add the base triangle last. Keep the leftover triangle square and triangle for another block or make blocks in pairs.

80 Japanese Arrow Feathers

[Size]
5in (12.7cm)

CUTTING LIST

A
B

- A   Four 1½ x 5½in (3.8 x 14cm) strips (see Making up)
- B   Two 1 x 5½in (2.5 x 14cm) strips

Making up

Use woven or printed wide stripes for the A strips. Cut them at 45 degrees to the stripes, offsetting stripes on adjacent strips to make a feather effect. Sew the block, using the diagram as a guide. Take care not to stretch bias edges as you sew.

81 Spool

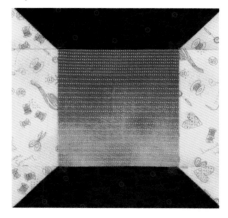

[Size]
5in (12.7cm)

CUTTING LIST

A
B

A One 3½in (8.9cm) square of striped fabric (see Making up)
B Two 1½ × 3½in (3.8cm × 8.9cm) strips
B Four 1½in (3.8cm) squares
C Two 5½ × 1½in (14 × 3.8cm) strips

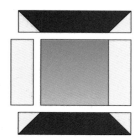

Making up
This block uses woven or printed narrow stripes for fabric A to suggest thread. Sew the block, using the diagram as a guide. Add the corner triangles to the 5½ × 1½in (14 × 3.8cm) strips using the 1½in (3.8cm) squares and the fast corners method (see page 23).

82 Pine Tree

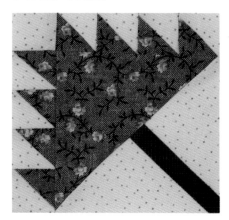

[Size]
5in (12.7cm)

CUTTING LIST

A
B

C

A One 3½ × 1in (8.9 × 2.5cm) strip
B One 4⅞in (12.4cm) square, quartered diagonally
B Four 1⅞in (4.8cm) squares
B One 1½in (3.8cm) square
C One 4⅞in (12.4cm) square, halved diagonally
C Four 1⅞in (4.8cm) squares

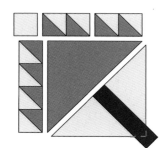

Making up
Sew the block, using the diagram as a guide. Using the 1⅞in (4.8cm) squares, make the triangle squares following the instructions on page 19. Sew the 3½ × 1in (8.9 × 2.5cm) strip between the two C triangles and trim the block corner, as shown by the dashed red line. Keep the remaining large triangles for another block or make blocks in pairs.

83 Sawtooth

[Size]
5in (12.7cm)

CUTTING LIST

A   Five 5½ ×1½in (14 × 3.8cm) strips
B   Ten 1½in (3.8cm) squares

Making up

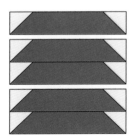

Sew the block, using the diagram as a guide. Add the triangles to the end of each strip using the fast corners method on page 23. If using fabric with a directional print, as shown here, make sure each strip is the right way up when adding the triangles.

Mix & Match
Quilt designs

The striking design above rotates Block 81 to create a central pattern and uses Blocks 80 and 82 for a border. A simple checkerboard with just two blocks would work well too. The example below uses Blocks 84 and 86.

84 Pointed Tile

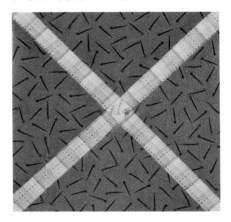

[Size]
5in (12.7cm)

CUTTING LIST

A   One 5½in (14cm) square, quartered diagonally
B   One 1in (2.5cm) square
C   Four 4 × 1in (10.2 × 2.5cm) strips

Making up

Sew the block, using the diagram as a guide. Sew the 4 × 1in (10.2 × 2.5cm) strips and the 1in (2.5cm) square between the A triangles and trim the block corners, as shown by the dashed red line. Blocks may be made in sets of four, with four different A fabrics and one triangle from each, for a scrap look.

85 Square on Point

[Size]
5in (12.7cm)

CUTTING LIST

A   One 5½in (14in) square
B   Four 3in (7.6cm) squares

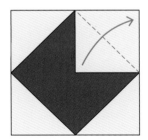

Making up

Sew the block, using the diagram as a guide. Use the fast corners method on page 23 to add the triangle corners.

86 Crossed Tile

[Size]
5in (12.7cm)

CUTTING LIST

 A

 B

 C

A   Two 3⅛in (7.9cm) squares
B   Two 3⅛in (7.9cm) squares
C   Two 2¾ × 1in (7 × 2.5cm) strips
C   One 5½ × 1in (14cm × 2.5cm) strip

Making up

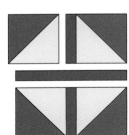

Sew the block, using the diagram as a guide. Use the triangle square method on page 19 to make the square units.

Mix & Match
Quilt designs

Block 83 lends itself to a continuous strippy arrangement, with Blocks 78 and 79 repeated in between in the design above. The little sampler panel on the left uses all the blocks in this chapter, arranging and rotating them for the best balance.

87 Dollhouse

[Size]
5in (12.7cm)

CUTTING LIST

A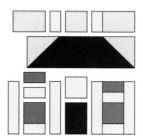

A Two 1½in (3.8cm) squares
A Two 1½ × 1in (3.8 × 2.5cm) strips
B One 2 × 1½in (5 × 3.8cm) strip
B One 2 × 5½in (5 × 14cm) strip
C Six 3 × 1in (7.6 × 2.5cm) strips
C Four 1½ × 1in (3.8 × 2.5cm) strips
C One 1½in (3.8cm) square
D One 1½in (3.8cm) square
D Two 2 × 1½in (5 × 3.8cm) strips
D Two 2½in (6.4cm) squares

A
B
C
D

Making up
Sew the block, using the diagram as a guide. Use the fast corners method on page 23 to add the triangle corners to the dollhouse "roof."

88 Sailboat

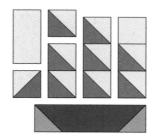

[Size]
5in (12.7cm)

CUTTING LIST

A One 5½ × 1¾in (14 × 4.4cm) strip
B Five 2⅛in (5.4cm) squares
C Two 1¾in (4.4cm) squares
D Five 2⅛in (5.4cm) squares
D One 3 × 1¾in (7.6 × 4.4cm) strip
D One 1¾in (4.4cm) square

A
B
D

Making up
Sew the block, using the diagram as a guide. Use the triangle square method on page 19 to make the "sails." Keep the spare triangle square for another block or make blocks in pairs. Use the fast corners method on page 23 to add the triangle corners to the "boat."

89 Arkansas Traveler Square

[Size]
5in (12.7cm)

CUTTING LIST

A
B

A One 6¼in (15.9cm) square, quartered diagonally
A One 3¾in (9.5cm) square, quartered diagonally
B Two pieces from template 37 (page 124)

Making up

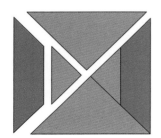

The Arkansas Traveler block is made from four finished squares, rotating alternate squares through 90 degrees. Sew the block, using the diagram as a guide. Keep the spare triangles for another block or make blocks in pairs.

PROJECT: PINCUSHION

Any block makes a pretty pincushion, an ideal gift for stitching friends. For 3in (7.6cm) or 4½in (11.4cm) blocks, add borders to make the block larger (see Adding borders, page 28) or make a smaller pincushion, cutting the backing square to fit the completed block of your choice.

YOU WILL NEED

One 5in (12.7cm) block of your choice
   (Block 79, Cake Stand, has been used here)
Two 1 × 5½in (2.5cm × 14cm) strips
Two 1 × 6½in (2.5 × 16.5cm) strips
One 6½in (16.5cm) square
Pieces of polyester batting, for stuffing

1 Sew the 1 × 5½in (2.5 × 14cm) strips to either side of the block of your choice and press toward the strips. Repeat with the two 1 × 6½in (2.5 × 16.5cm) strips.

2 Place the pincushion top and the 6½in (16.5cm) square right sides together. Machine-sew all round, starting and finishing with a few backstitches and leaving a 3in (7.6cm) gap unsewn on one side. Turn the pincushion right side out through the gap. Make sure the corners are turned out well.

3 Stuff the pincushion firmly, teasing out the pieces of batting to avoid lumps. Slip-stich the gap closed.

Japanese Odyssey

Japanese fabrics and motifs can add a rich and unusual style to your patchwork. These blocks combine classical geometric motifs, architectural designs, and objects associated with Japan to showcase a variety of colorful fabrics, often with metallic gold accents. Contrast large and small motifs, or use fabrics for realistic effects, such as the roof and background for the Pagoda block (page 98). Large prints work well for blocks like Kimono (page 96) and Fan Paper (page 99). To make the blocks in this section, a charm pack with 6in (15.2cm) squares was combined with scraps left over from other projects. The metallic gold overprinting featured on many of the fabrics helps to unify the scraps. The finished block size is 5in (12.7cm).

90 Octagon

[Size]
5in (12.7cm)

A

B

CUTTING LIST

A   One 5½in (14cm) square
B   Four 1½in (3.8cm) squares

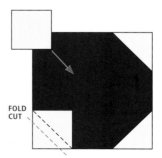

FOLD
CUT

Making up

Sew the block, using the diagram as a guide. Add the corner triangles using the 1½in (3.8cm) squares and the fast corners method (see page 23).

91 Five Strips

[Size]
5in (12.7cm)

CUTTING LIST

A
B
C
D
E

A   One 12 × 1in (30.5 × 2.5cm) strip
B   One 12 × 1in (30.5 × 2.5cm) strip
C   One 12 × 1in (30.5 × 2.5cm) strip
D   One 12 × 1in (30.5 × 2.5cm) strip
E   One 12 × 1in (30.5 × 2.5cm) strip

Making up

Sew all five strips together and press. Cut four 3 × 3in (7.6 × 7.6cm) squares from the patchwork strip. Sew the block, using the diagram as a guide. The block can also be made from 20 individual 3 × 1in (7.6 × 2.5cm) strips.

92 Irori (hearth)

[Size]
5in (12.7cm)

CUTTING LIST

A
B

A   Four 2 × 4in (5cm × 10.2cm) strips
B   One 2½in (6.4cm) square

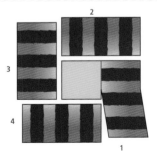

Making up

Sew the block, using the diagram as a guide. The block is assembled from the center outward. Sew only 1½in (3.8cm) of the first seam, as highlighted in red. Press all seams toward the edge of the block. Sew the next strip across the top of the block, then sew the other two strips in sequence. Finish by completing the first seam, overlapping the stitching line by about ½in (1.3cm).

93 Igeta (well curb)

[Size]
5in (12.7cm)

CUTTING LIST

A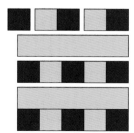

B

A   Six 1½in (3.8cm) squares
A   Two 1½ × 5½in (3.8 × 14cm) strips
B   Nine 1½in (3.8cm) squares

Making up

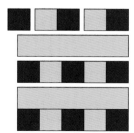

Sew the block, using the diagram as a guide. The block is assembled in strips.

94 Masu (measuring boxes)

[Size]
5in (12.7cm)

CUTTING LIST

A

B

C

A   One 1½in (3.8cm) square
B   Two 1½in (3.8cm) squares
B   Two 3½ × 1½in (8.9 × 3.8cm) strips
C   Two 3½ × 1½in (8.9 × 3.8cm) strips
C   Two 5½ × 1½in (14 × 3.8cm) strips

Making up

Sew the block, using the diagram as a guide. The block is assembled from the center outward.

95 Eight Tatami (mats)

[Size]
5in (12.7cm)

CUTTING LIST

A   Eight 3 × 1¾in (7.6 × 4.4cm) strips
of a large-print fabric

Making up
Using a large print for this block
helps to emphasize the seams.
Sew the block, using the diagram
as a guide. The block is assembled
from the center outward.

Mix & Match
Quilt designs

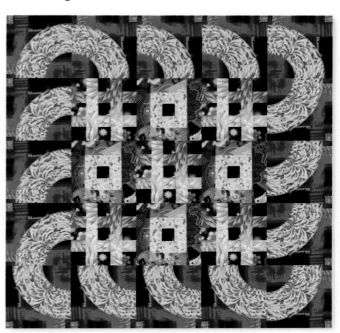

The checkerboard design above
uses two geometric blocks, 93
and 94, for the center, with Block
102, rotated, creating a dynamic
border pattern. In the wall hanging
on the left, pictorial Blocks 98, 99,
101, 97, and 96 alternate with
Block 100.

96 Kimono

[Size]
5in (12.7cm)

CUTTING LIST

A

B

A   Two 5 × 1¾in (12.7 × 4.4cm) strips
A   Two 2½ × 1¾in (6.4 × 4.4cm) strips
A   One ¾ × 1½in (1.9 × 3.8cm) strip
A   One piece from template 43 (page 125)
A   One piece from template 43 (page 125), flipped
B   One 5½ × ¾in (14 × 1.9cm) strip
B   Two 3 × 1¾in (7.6 × 4.4cm) strips

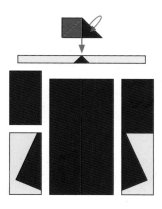

Making up

Turn under ¼in (6mm) along the two sloping edges of pieces cut from template 43. Appliqué one piece to each 3 × 1¾in (7.6 × 4.4cm) strip (see page 25). Sew the ¾ × 1½in (1.9 × 3.8cm) strip as shown and appliqué to the center of the 5½ × ¾in (14 × 1.9cm) strip, for the collar. Sew the block, using the diagram as a guide. The block is assembled from the center outward.

97 Moon over Mountain

[Size]
5in (12.7cm)

CUTTING LIST

A

B

C

A   One 5½in (14cm) square
B   One 2½in (6.4cm) diameter circle
C   One 3¾in (9.5cm) square, halved diagonally

Making up

Use the fused (bonded) appliqué method to apply the circle to the center of the block (see page 25). Press under ¼in (6mm) along the two shorter sides of one triangle and appliqué to the block. Keep the remaining triangle to make another block.

98 Chochin (lantern)

[Size]
5in (12.7cm)

CUTTING LIST

 A

 B

 C

A	One 4½ × 1½in (11.4 × 3.8cm) strip
A	Two 4 × 1in (10.2 × 2.5cm) strips
A	Two 3½ × 1in (8.9 × 2.5cm) strips
A	Two 3 × 1in (7.6 × 2.5cm) strips
B	Two 2 × 1in (5 × 2.5cm) strips
C	Four 1in (2.5cm) strips in the following lengths: 2¼in (5.7cm), 1¾in (4.4cm), 1½in (3.8cm), and 1¼in (3.2cm)
C	Two 1½ × 1in (3.8cm × 2.5cm) strips

99 Torii (shrine gate)

[Size]
5in (12.7cm)

CUTTING LIST

A

B

A	One 5½ × 1in (14 × 2.5cm) strip
A	One 5½ × 4½in (14 × 11.4cm) strip
B	One 5½ × 1in (14 × 2.5cm) strip
B	One 1in (2.5cm) square
B	One 3 × 1in (7.6 × 2.5cm) strip
B	Two 5 × 1in (12.7cm × 2.5cm) strips

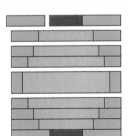

Making up

Sew the block, using the diagram as a guide. The block is assembled in strips.

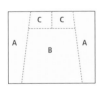

Making up

Cut the 5½ × 4½in (14 × 11.4cm) strip as shown by the dashed lines. Cut sloping vertical lines from 1in (2.5cm) along the base line, tapering to 1½in (3.8cm) along the top (A). Cut horizontally across the center section 1in (2.5cm) from the top (B). Cut the small top center section in half vertically (C). Rejoin the pieces using the 1in- (2.5cm-) wide B strips like sashing, as shown, starting with the smallest piece and trimming the strip ends as you go.

100 Masumon Square Pattern

[Size]
5in (12.7cm)

CUTTING LIST

A
B
C

A   Two 5½ × 1¾in (14 × 4.4cm) strips
A   Two 3 × 1¾in (7.6 × 4.4cm) strips
B   Two 1¾in (4.4cm) squares
C   Two 1¾in (4.4cm) squares

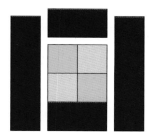

Making up

Sew the block, using the diagram as a guide. Construct the central Four Patch first (see page 44), then add the border pieces.

101 Pagoda

[Size]
5in (12.7cm)

CUTTING LIST

A
B
C
D

A   Two 5½ × 1½in (14 × 3.8cm) strips
B   One 3½ × ¾in (8.9 × 1.9cm) strip
B   Four 1½ × 1in (3.8 × 2.5cm) strips
B   Two 1¼ × 1in (3.2cm × 2.5cm) strips
B   Two 1¼in (3.2cm) squares
B   One piece from templates 40 and 42 (page 125)
B   One piece from templates above, flipped
B   Two 1½ × 1in (3.8 × 2.5cm) strips
B   Two ¾in (1.9cm) squares
C   One 3½ × 1¼in (8.9 × 3.2cm) strip
C   One piece from template 39 (page 125)
C   One piece from template 41 (page 125)
D   Three strips: 1½ × 1in (3.8 × 2.5cm), 2 × 1in (5 × 2.5cm) 1½ × 2½in (3.8 × 6.4cm)
D   One ¾in- (1.9cm-) wide strip in the following lengths: 3½in (8.9cm), 3in (7.6cm)

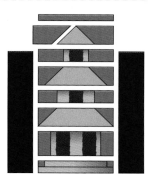

Making up

Sew the block, using the diagram as a guide. Use the fast corners method (see page 23) to add the 1¼in (3.2cm) squares to the 3½ × 1¼in (8.9 × 3.2cm) strip.

Fan Paper

[Size]
5in (12.7cm)

CUTTING LIST

A

A   One 5½in (14cm) square
B   One piece from template 38 (page 125)

Making up

Assemble the block, using the diagram as a guide. Appliqué the fan paper motif using the fused (bonded) appliqué method (see page 25).

PROJECT: BOOK BAG

Follow the instructions on page 32 to make this neat book bag, perfect for your holiday or commuter reading. It is 9in (22.9cm) tall x 12in (30.5cm) wide which will fit most thick paperback novels. The handles are made from 12 × 2½in (20.5cm × 6.4cm) strips (see page 32).

Use two 5½in (14cm) (unfinished size) blocks and machine-sew a 2 × 5½in (5 × 14cm) strip to the top and bottom of each block. Join the blocks with a 2½ × 9½in (6.4 x 24cm) strip.

The lining fabric is 9½ × 12½in (24 × 31.8cm). The folded pocket panels are 9½ (24cm) squares folded in half and machine-sewn ⅛in (3mm) from the folded edge.

The pocket panels, handles and lining are layered and sewn as described in steps 3 and 4 on page 33.

Country Classics

Many classic American quilt blocks make gorgeous mini blocks. Many are very well known with traditional names reflecting everyday items, events in the news, or biblical references. A pretty charm pack in the red and green colorway so popular for late nineteenth-century quilts gives plenty of fabric variety for an authentic scrap look. Because 5in (12.7cm) charms limit the number of pieces that can be cut from each fabric, match up similar fabrics and make two-color blocks with four or more prints, mixing in a few fat quarters for backgrounds to unify the blocks, just as the quilters of yesteryear did.

103 Single Irish Chain

[Size]
5in (12.7cm)

CUTTING LIST

A
B

A   Four 1½ × 3½in (3.8 × 8.9cm) strips
A   Four 1½in (3.8cm) squares
B   Nine 1½in (3.8cm) squares

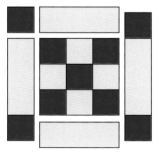

Making up

Sew the block, using the diagram as a guide. Construct the block center, following the Nine Patch instructions (see page 68). Add the remaining four 1½in (3.8cm) squares and the 1½ × 3½in (3.8 × 8.9cm) strips, as shown in the diagram. For a traditional Single Irish Chain pattern, alternate blocks with unpieced 5½in (14cm) A squares.

104 Double Irish Chain 1

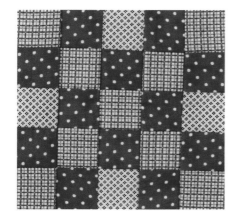

[Size]
5in (12.7cm)

	CUTTING LIST
A	A Four 1½in (3.8cm) squares
B	B Nine 1½in (3.8cm) squares
C	C Twelve 1½in (3.8cm) squares

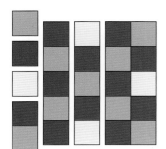

Making up

Sew the block, using the diagram as a guide. Sew the pieces together into strips, then sew strips together to complete the block. This block alternates with Double Irish Chain 2 to make the traditional Double Irish Chain pattern.

105 Double Irish Chain 2

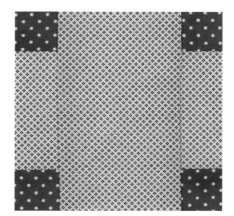

[Size]
5in (12.7cm)

	CUTTING LIST
A	A One 5½ × 3½in (14 × 8.9cm) strip
B	A Two 3½ × 1½in (8.9 × 3.8cm) strips
	B Four 1½in (3.8cm) squares

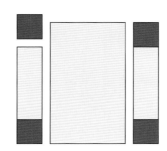

Making up

Sew the block, using the diagram as a guide. Sew the pieces together into strips, then sew strips together to complete the block. This block alternates with Double Irish Chain 1 to make the traditional Double Irish Chain pattern.

106 Sister's Choice

[Size]
5in (12.7cm)

CUTTING LIST

 A

 B

 C

D

A   Eight 1½in (3.8cm) squares
B   Nine 1½in (3.8cm) squares
C   Four 1⅞in (4.8cm) squares
D   Four 1⅞in (4.8cm) squares

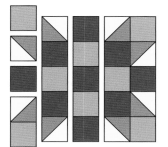

Making up
Sew the block, using the diagram as a guide. Using the 1⅞in (4.8cm) squares, make triangle squares (see page 19). Assemble the block in strips.

107 Cain and Abel

[Size]
5in (12.7cm)

CUTTING LIST

A

B

C

A   Nine 1½in (3.8cm) squares
A   Four 1⅞in (4.8cm) squares
B   Four 1½in (3.8cm) squares
C   Four 1½in (3.8cm) squares
C   Four 1⅞in (4.8cm) squares

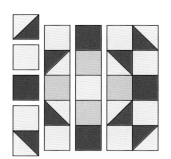

Making up
Sew the block, using the diagram as a guide. Using the 1⅞in (4.8cm) squares, make triangle squares (see page 19). Assemble the block in strips.

108

Double Wrench

[Size]
5in (12.7cm)

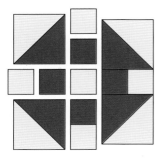

Making up

Sew the block, using the diagram as a guide. Using the 2⅞in (7.3cm) squares, make triangle squares (see page 19). Sew the pieces together into strips, then sew strips together to complete the block.

Mix & Match

Quilt designs

Two different blocks can be combined in a checkerboard arrangement, which is good for scrap quilts. Blocks 104 and 105 combine to create the Double Irish Chain above, while the checkerboard arrangement below is made up from Blocks 113 and 114.

109 Puss in the Corner

[Size]
5in (12.7cm)

A

B

C

CUTTING LIST

A   Four 1¾ × 3in (4.4 × 7.6cm) strips

A   Two 2⅛in (5.4cm) squares

B   One 3in (7.6cm) square

C   Two 2⅛in (5.4cm) squares

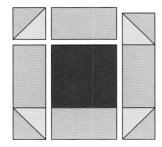

Making up

Sew the block, using the diagram as a guide. Using the 2⅛in (5.4cm) squares, make triangle squares (see page 19). Sew the pieces together into strips, then sew the strips together to complete the block.

110 Delectable Mountains

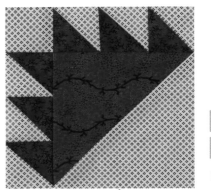

[Size]
5in (12.7cm)

A

B

C

CUTTING LIST

A   Three 2⅛in (5.4cm) squares

A   One 1¾in (4.4cm) square

A   One 4⅝in (11.7cm) square

B   Three 2⅛in (5.4cm) squares

C   One 4⅝in (11.7cm) square

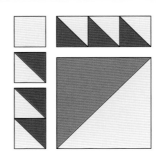

Making up

Sew the block, using the diagram as a guide. Using the 2⅛in (5.4cm) and 4⅝in (11.7cm) squares, make triangle squares (see page 19). Sew the smaller triangle squares together into strips, then sew strips to the larger triangle squares. Keep the remaining large triangle square for another block.

111 Three-color Economy

[Size]
5in (12.7cm)

		CUTTING LIST
A		A One 3in (7.6cm) square
B		B One 3¾in (9.5cm) square, quartered diagonally
C		C Two 3⅜in (8.6cm) squares, halved diagonally

Making up

Sew the block, using the diagram as a guide. Assemble the block from the center outward.

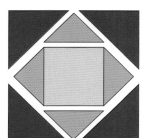

112 Right and Left

[Size]
5in (12.7cm)

		CUTTING LIST
A		A One 4in (10.2cm) square
B		B One 3¾in (9.5cm) square, quartered diagonally
C		C One 3¾in (9.5cm) square, quartered diagonally

Making up

Sew the block, using the diagram as a guide. Arrange and sew the corner triangle pairs. Assemble the block from the center outward.

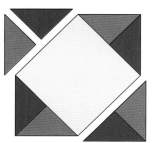

113 Friendship Variation

[Size]
5in (12.7cm)

CUTTING LIST

A
B
C
D

A   Two pieces from template 44 (page 125)
B   Two pieces from template 44 (page 125)
C   One 1⅝in (4.1cm) square, halved diagonally
C   One 3⅜in (8.6cm) square, halved diagonally
D   One 1⅝in (4.1cm) square, halved diagonally
D   One 3⅜in (8.6cm) square, halved diagonally

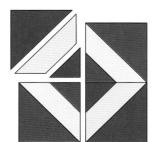

Making up
Sew the block, using the diagram as a guide. Sew the triangles and strips together to make squares. Assemble the block as a Four Patch (see page 44).

114 Fancy Stripe Variation

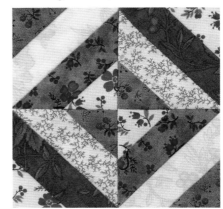

[Size]
5in (12.7cm)

CUTTING LIST

A
B
C
D
E

A   Two pieces from template 44 (page 125)
B   Two pieces from template 44 (page 125)
C   Two 1⅝in (4.1cm) squares, halved diagonally
D   Two pieces from template 44 (page 125)
E   Two pieces from template 44 (page 125)
E   Two 1⅝in (4.1cm) squares, halved diagonally

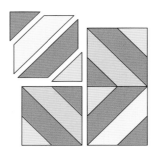

Making up
Sew the block, using the diagram as a guide. Sew the triangles and strips together to make squares. Assemble the block as a Four Patch (see page 44).

115

Flying Dutchman

[Size]
5in (12.7cm)

CUTTING LIST

A   Sixteen 1¾in (4.4cm) squares
B   Two 3 × 1¾in (7.6 × 4.4cm) strips
C   Two 3 × 1¾in (7.6 × 4.4cm) strips
D   Two 3 × 1¾in (7.6 × 4.4cm) strips
E   Two 3 × 1¾in (7.6 × 4.4cm) strips

Making up

Sew the block, using the diagram as a guide. Make eight Flying Geese units (see page 55). Sew two units together to make a square. Assemble the block as a Four Patch (see page 44).

Mix & Match
Quilt designs

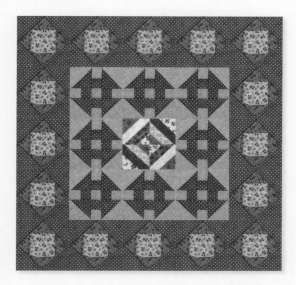

A simple medallion arrangement works well with traditional blocks. Block 114 forms the center of the design above, surrounded by Block 108 with Block 111 as a border. Stripey layouts, like the one below, can produce some interesting secondary patterns where blocks meet. Rows of Blocks 106 and 107 have been used here. Notice how the horizontal stripes of the two blocks meet, giving the design overall coherence.

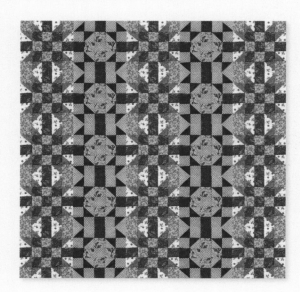

116 Northern Lights

[Size]
5in (12.7cm)

CUTTING LIST

A   One 3⅜in (8.6cm) square
B   One 3⅜in (8.6cm) square
C   Four 1¾in (4.4cm) squares
D   Four 1¾in (4.4cm) squares

117 Checkerboard

[Size]
5in (12.7cm)

CUTTING LIST

A   Eight 1¾in (4.4cm) squares of dark fabric
B   Eight 1¾in (4.4cm) squares of light fabric

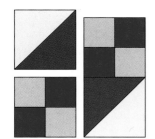

Making up

Sew the block, using the diagram as a guide. Using the 1¾in (4.4cm) squares, make two Four Patch units (page 44). Use the larger squares to make two triangle squares (page 19). Assemble the block in strips.

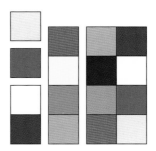

Making up

Sew the block, using the diagram as a guide. Arrange the squares, alternating between light and dark fabrics, for a checkerboard effect. Include some darker lights and lighter dark prints for variety, or use up scraps left over from the other blocks. This block can also be made using the Seminole patchwork method on page 22.

Project: Potholder

Mom's favorite and a really easy make,
a potholder needs just one block and
a few remnants. If you want your potholder
to be practical as well as pretty, use a
thermal batting to keep your hand cool.

YOU WILL NEED

One 5in (12.7cm) block of your choice
Inner border
Two 5½ × 1½in (14 × 3.8cm) strips
Two 7½ × 1½in (19 × 3.8cm) strips
Outer border
Two 7½ × 1½in (19 × 3.8cm) strips
Two 9½ × 1½in (24 × 3.8cm) strips
One 9½in (24cm) square, for backing
One 9½in (24cm) square of batting
One 1½ × 5in strip (3.8 × 12.7cm) strip,
for hanging loop

1 Machine-sew the borders to the block and
press. Press the 5in × 1½in (12.7cm × 3.8cm)
strip in half along the length and open out the
fold. Fold the raw edges to match the center crease
and press again. Machine-sew along each long side
to make the hanging loop. Fold the loop, crossing
over the ends, and baste ends in place.

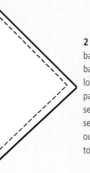

2 With the patchwork panel, batting, and
backing, layer the potholder ready for
bagging out (see page 29). Place the hanging
loop in one corner, as shown, between the
patchwork panel and the backing. Machine-
sew around the potholder with a ½in (1.3cm)
seam, following the instructions on bagging
out. Machine- or hand-quilt a simple design
to secure the layers.

Log Cabin

There are many variations on the strip block known to quilters as Log Cabin. Antique Log Cabin quilts often use small blocks and narrow strips, so here the block is returning to its roots. The contrasting center present in most Log Cabin designs is usually the same color throughout the quilt; red, yellow, white, or black were popular choices. Here, this is updated with central squares in a vivid lime green, as well as lime green triangles. Log Cabin blocks need contrasting strips, so try varying pattern and color, as well as the light and dark values. As different blocks include various strip widths, a coordinated pack of 10in (25.4cm) squares provides a very economical fabric source with a fresh, modern style, but you can use any fabrics you like. Cut the longest strips first—shorter strips can be cut from leftover pieces. The finished blocks are 5in (12.7cm).

118 Courthouse Steps

[Size]
5in (12.7cm)

CUTTING LIST

A   A   One 1½in (3.8cm) square

B   B   Two 1in- (2.5cm-) wide strips in each of these lengths: 4½in (11.4cm), 3½in (8.9cm), 2½in (6.4cm), 1½in (3.8cm)

C   C   Two 1in- (2.5cm-) wide strips in each of these lengths: 5½in (14cm), 4½in (11.4cm), 3½in (8.9cm), 2½in (6.4cm)

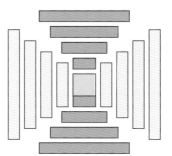

Making up

Sew the block, using the diagram as a guide and working outward from the center. Take care to keep accurate ¼in (6mm) seam allowances.

119 Four-color Courthouse Steps

[Size]
5in (12.7cm)

CUTTING LIST

 A

 B

 C

D

E

A One 1½in (3.8cm) square
B One 1in- (2.5cm-) wide strip in each of these lengths:
4½in (11.4cm), 3½in (8.9cm), 2½in (6.4cm),1½in (3.8cm)
C One 1in- (2.5cm-) wide strip in each of these lengths:
4½in (11.4cm), 3½in (8.9cm), 2½in (6.4cm),1½in (3.8cm)
D One 1in- (2.5cm-) wide strip in each of these lengths:
5½in (14cm), 4½in (11.4cm), 3½in (8.9cm), 2½in (6.4cm)

Making up

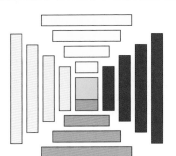

Sew the block, using the diagram as a guide and working outward from the center. Take care to keep accurate ¼in (6mm) seam allowances.

120 Striped Log Cabin

[Size]
5in (12.7cm)

CUTTING LIST

 A

 B

 C

 D

 E

A One 1½in (3.8cm) square
B One 1in- (2.5cm-) wide strip in each of these lengths:
4½in (11.4cm), 3½in (8.9cm), 2in (5cm), 1½in (3.8cm)
C One 1in- (2.5cm-) wide strip in each of these lengths:
5in (12.7cm), 4½in (11.4cm), 3in (7.6cm), 2½in (6.4cm)
D One 1in- (2.5cm-) wide strip in each of these lengths:
4½in (11.4cm), 4in (10.2cm), 2½in (6.4cm), 2in (5cm)
E One 1in- (2.5cm-) wide strip in each of these lengths:
5½in (14cm), 5in (12.7cm), 3½in (8.9cm), 3in (7.6cm)

Making up

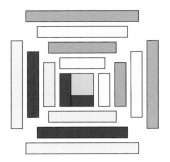

Sew the block, using the diagram as a guide and working outward from the center. Take care to keep accurate ¼in (6mm) seam allowances.

121 Log Cabin

[Size]
5in (12.7cm)

CUTTING LIST

 A

B

C

A   One 1½in (3.8cm) square
B   One 1in- (2.5cm-) wide strip in each of these lengths:
    5in (12.7cm), 4½in (11.4cm), 4in (10.2cm), 3½in (8.9cm),
    3in (7.6cm), 2½in (6.4cm), 2in (5cm), 1½in (3.8cm)
C   One 1in- (2.5cm-) wide strip in each of these lengths:
    5½in (14cm), 5in (12.7cm), 4½in (11.4cm), 4in (10.2cm),
    3½in (8.9cm), 3in (7.6cm), 2½in (6.4cm), 2in (5cm)

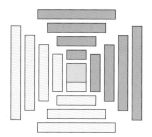

Making up

Sew the block, using the diagram as a guide and working outward from the center. Take care to keep accurate ¼in (6mm) seam allowances.

122 Wild Geese

[Size]
5in (12.7cm)

CUTTING LIST

A

B

C

A   Seventeen 1½in (3.8cm) squares
B   Two 1in- (2.5cm-) wide strips in each of these lengths:
    4½in (11.4cm), 3½in (8.9cm), 2½in (6.4cm), 1½in (3.8cm)
C   Two 1in- (2.5cm-) wide strips in each of these lengths:
    5½in (14cm), 4½in (11.4cm), 3½in (8.9cm), 2½in (6.4cm)

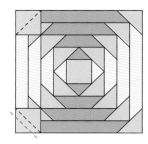

Making up

Sew the block, using the diagram as a guide and working outward from the center. Take care to keep accurate ¼in (6mm) seam allowances. Sew each round of strips following the instructions for Courthouse Steps (see page 111). After each round, add four corner triangles using the fast corners method on page 19. The diagram shows how the last set of corner triangles are sewn.

123 Corner in the Cabin

[Size]
5in (12.7cm)

CUTTING LIST

 A

 B

 C

A One 1½in (3.8cm) square
B One 1in- (2.5cm-) wide strip in each of these lengths:
   5in (12.7cm), 4½in (11.4cm), 4in (10.2cm), 3½in (8.9cm),
   3in (7.6cm), 2½in (6.4cm), 2cm (5cm), 1½in (3.8cm)
C One 1in- (2.5cm-) wide strip in each of these lengths:
   5½in (14cm), 5in (12.7cm), 4½in (11.4cm), 4in (10.2cm),
   3½in (8.9cm), 3in (7.6cm), 2½in (6.4cm), 2cm (5cm)

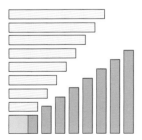

Making up

Sew the block, using the diagram as a guide and working outward from the corner square. Take care to keep accurate ¼in (6mm) seam allowances.

Mix & Match
Quilt designs

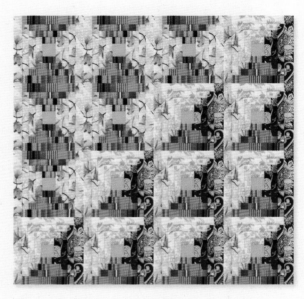

Try coordinating fabrics with two block designs. In the example above, Blocks 118 and 119 are arranged with a diagonal split across the patchwork while alternating and rotating Blocks 120 and 121 gives the optical effect of a wave below.

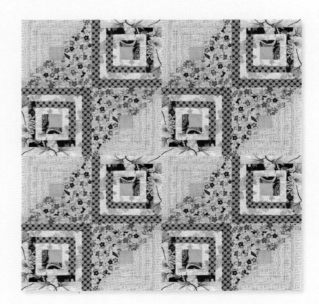

124 Double Spiral

[Size]
5in (12.7cm)

CUTTING LIST

 A
 B
 C

A   One 1½in (3.8cm) square
B   One 5½ × 1in (14 × 2.5cm) strip
B   One 1½ × 1in (3.8 × 2.5cm) strip
B   Two 1in- (2.5cm-) wide strips in each of these lengths:
    4½in (11.4cm), 3½in (8.9cm), 2½in (6.4cm)
C   One 5½ × 1in (14 × 2.5cm) strip
C   One 1½ × 1in (3.8 × 2.5cm) strip
C   Two 1in- (2.5cm-) wide strips in each of these lengths:
    4½in (11.4cm), 3½in (8.9cm), 2½in (6.4cm)

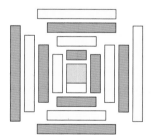

Making up

Sew the block, using the diagram as a guide and working outward from the center square. Arrange the pieces to make a double spiral. Take care to keep accurate ¼in (6mm) seam allowances.

125 Wide and Narrow Spiral

[Size]
5in (12.7cm)

CUTTING LIST

A
B

A   One 1¼in (3.2cm) square
A   One 1¼in- (3.2cm-) wide strip in each of these lengths:
    5in (12.7cm), 4¼in (10.8cm), 3¾in (9.5cm), 3in (7.6cm),
    2½in (6.4cm), 1¾in (4.4cm)
B   One 1in- (2.5cm-) wide strip in each of these lengths:
    5½in (14cm), 5in (12.7cm), 4¼in (10.8cm), 3¾in (9.5cm),
    3in (7.6cm), 2½in (6.4cm), 1¾in (4.4cm), 1¼in (3.2cm)

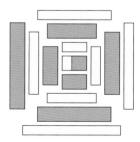

Making up

Sew the block, using the diagram as a guide and working outward from the center square. Arrange the pieces to make a double spiral. Take care to keep accurate ¼in (6mm) seam allowances.

126 Curved Log Cabin

[Size]
5in (12.7cm)

CUTTING LIST

 A

 B

A   One 1¼in (3.2cm) square

A   One 1¼in- (3.2cm-) wide strip in each of these lengths:
5in (12.7cm), 4¼in (10.8cm), 3¾in (9.5cm), 3in (7.6cm),
2½in (6.4cm), 1¾in (4.4cm)

B   One 1in- (2.5cm-) wide strip in each of these lengths:
5½in (14cm), 5in (12.7cm), 4¼in (10.8cm), 3¾in (9.5cm),
3in (7.6cm), 2½in (6.4cm), 1¾in (4.4cm), 1¼in (3.2cm)

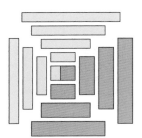

Making up

Sew the block, using the
diagram as a guide and
working outward from the
center square. Take care to
keep accurate ¼in (6mm)
seam allowances.

127 Nine-patch Log Cabin

[Size]
5in (12.7cm)

CUTTING LIST

A

B

C

D

A   Four 1in (2.5cm) squares

B   Five 1in (2.5cm) squares

C   One 1in- (2.5cm-) wide strip in each of these lengths:
4in (10.2cm), 3½in (8.9cm), 3in (7.6cm), 2½in (6.4cm)

C   One 1¼ × 4¾in (3.2 × 12cm) strip

C   One 1¼ × 5½in (3.2 × 14cm) strip

D   One 1in- (2.5cm-) wide strip in each of these lengths:
3½in (8.9cm), 3in (7.6cm), 2½in (6.4cm), 2in (5cm)

D   One 1¼ × 4in (3.2 × 10.2cm) strip

D   One 1¼ × 4¾in (3.2 × 12cm) strip

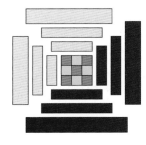

Making up

Make the Nine Patch center using
fabrics A and B (see Nine Patch 1,
page 68). Sew the block, using the
diagram as a guide and working
outward from the center Nine
Patch. Take care to keep accurate
¼in (6mm) seam allowances.

128 Cornerstones

[Size]
5in (12.7cm)

A
B
C

CUTTING LIST

A One 1½in (3.8cm) square
A Sixteen 1in (2.5cm) squares
B Two 1in- (2.5cm-) wide strips in each of these lengths:
4½in (11.4cm), 3½in (8.9cm), 2½in (6.4cm), 1½in (3.8cm)
C Two 1in- (2.5cm-) wide strips in each of these lengths:
4½in (11.4cm), 3½in (8.9cm), 2½in (6.4cm), 1½in (3.8cm)

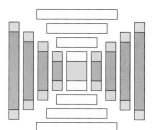

Making up

Sew the block, using the diagram as a guide and working outward from the center square. Take care to keep accurate ¼in (6mm) seam allowances.

129 Chimneys and Cornerstones

[Size]
5in (12.7cm)

A
B
C
D

CUTTING LIST

A Ten 1in (2.5cm) squares
B Two 1in (2.5cm) squares
C One 1in- (2.5cm-) wide strip in each of these lengths:
5in (12.7cm), 4½in (11.4cm), 4in (10.2cm), 3½in (8.9cm),
3in (7.6cm), 2½in (6.4cm), 2in (5cm), 1½in (3.8cm)
C One 1in- (2.5cm-) wide strip in each of these lengths:
5in (12.7cm), 4½in (11.4cm), 4in (10.2cm), 3½in (8.9cm),
3in (7.6cm), 2½in (6.4cm), 2in (5cm), 1½in (3.8cm)

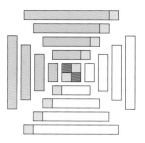

Making up

Make the Four Patch center using fabrics A and B (see Four Patch, page 44). Sew the block, using the diagram as a guide and working outward from the center Four Patch. Take care to keep accurate ¼in (6mm) seam allowances.

130 Cabin in the Cotton

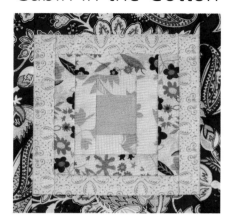

[Size]
5in (12.7cm)

CUTTING LIST

A   One 1½in (3.8cm) square
B   Two 1 × 1½in (2.5 × 3.8cm) strips
B   Two 1 × 2½in (2.5 × 6.4cm) strips
C   Two 1 × 2½in (2.5 × 6.4cm) strips
C   Two 1 × 3½in (2.5 × 8.9cm) strips
D   Two 1 × 3½in (2.5cm × 8.9cm) strips
D   Two 1 × 4½in (2.5cm × 11.4cm) strips
E   Two 1 × 4½in (2.5cm × 11.4cm) strips
E   Two 1 × 5½in (2.5 × 14cm) strips

A
B
B
C
C
D
D
E
E

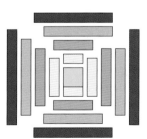

Making up

Sew the block, using the diagram as a guide and working outward from the center. Take care to keep accurate ¼in (6mm) seam allowances.

Mix & Match
Quilt designs

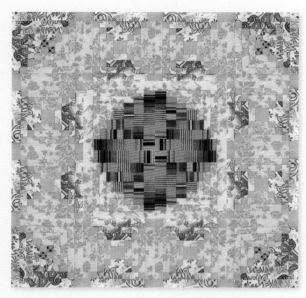

Blocks 128 and 129, rotated, make a continuous border around four of Blocks 126, rotated to create a central circle, above. If you prefer an asymmetrical design like the one below, try mixing different blocks in a random arrangement, matching some fabrics from one block to another to create an abstract design.

Templates

Where patchwork or appliqué shapes would be difficult to cut directly with a quilter's ruler, templates are needed. All the templates used in this book are on the following pages, grouped by chapter heading.

Working with templates

The template reference number and page number are given in the block cutting lists.

A few templates are used in more than one block; the reference number relates to the first block where they are used.

All of the templates are shown actual size.

Trace or photocopy the templates you need for the block. Pin the templates to the fabric.

A double-headed arrow on the template shows the direction of the fabric grain where it is important.

The gray templates on page 124 should be cut from paper for English paper piecing (page 21).

Patchwork—All patchwork templates have a ¼in (6 mm) seam allowance already added. The solid black line indicates the cutting line; the dashed black line within shows the sewing line.

Appliqué—Draw around the edge of the paper with a contrasting fabric marker or pencil. Cut out the pieces.

See page 19 for more information about cutting out and using templates.

Retro Revival

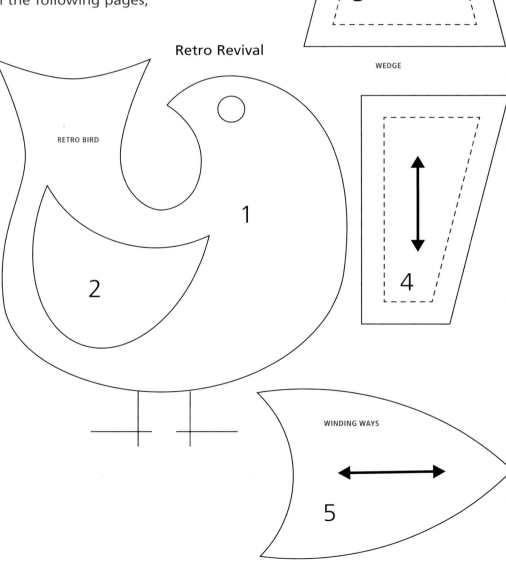

RETRO BIRD

WEDGE

WINDING WAYS

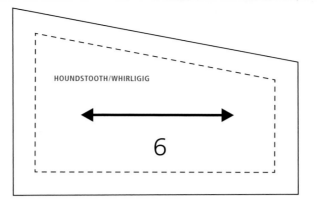

HOUNDSTOOTH/WHIRLIGIG

6

ROBBING PETER TO PAY PAUL

Center cross and arc are cut
from one 5½in (13.9cm)
square; arcs used for one
block and center cross for
another.

7

Retro Revival continued

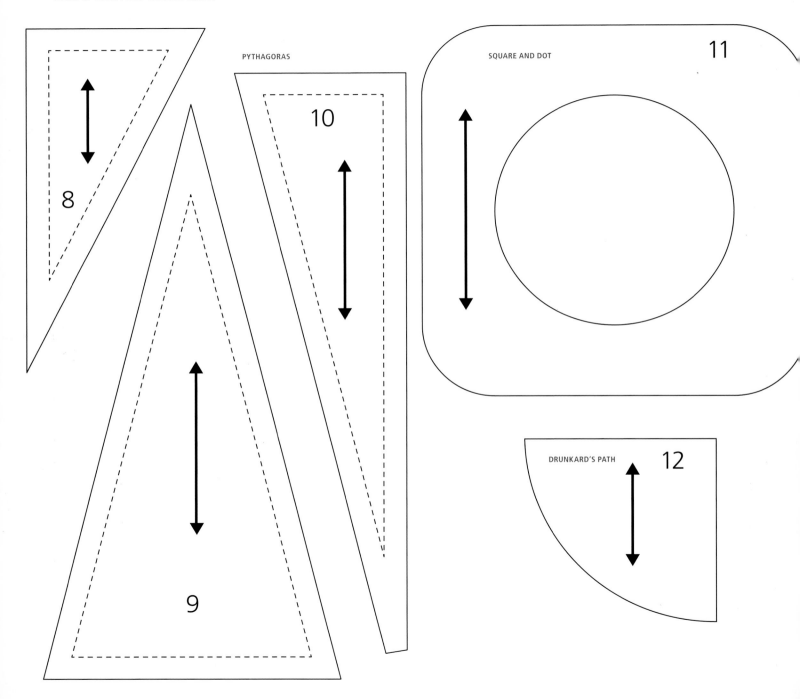

PYTHAGORAS

8

9

10

SQUARE AND DOT

11

DRUNKARD'S PATH

12

Thrifty Thirties

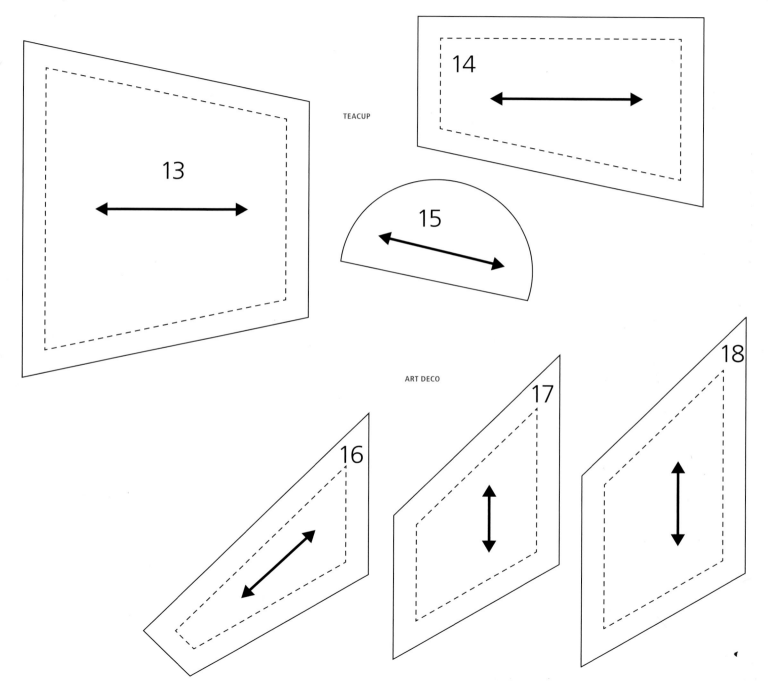

TEACUP

ART DECO

Thrifty Thirties continued

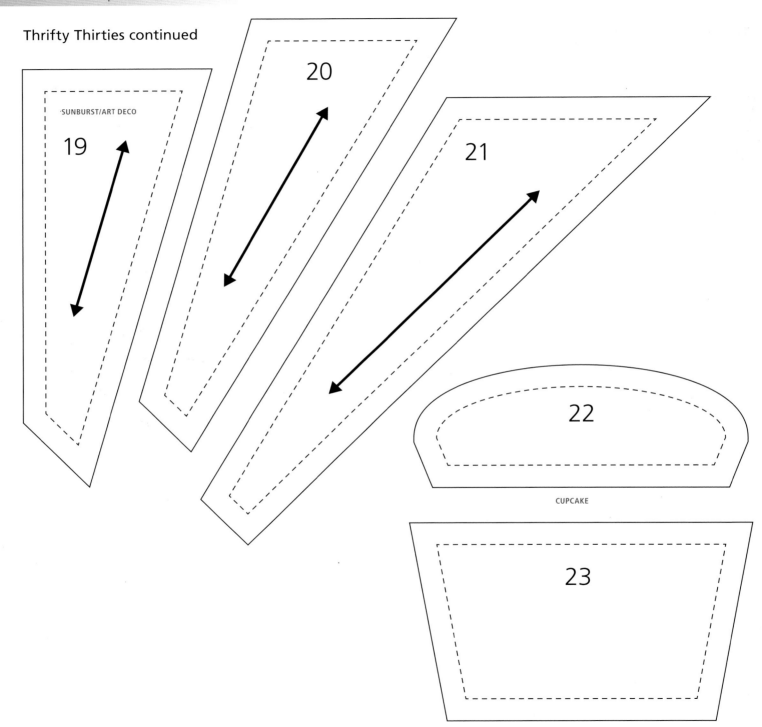

SUNBURST/ART DECO

19

20

21

22

CUPCAKE

23

Thrifty Thirties continued

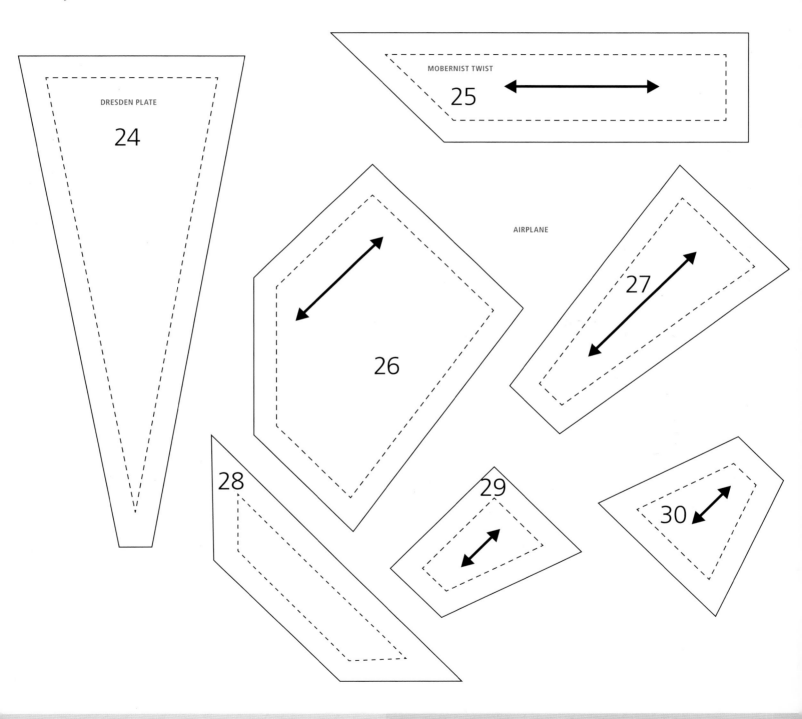

DRESDEN PLATE

24

MOBERNIST TWIST

25

AIRPLANE

26

27

28

29

30

English Traditions

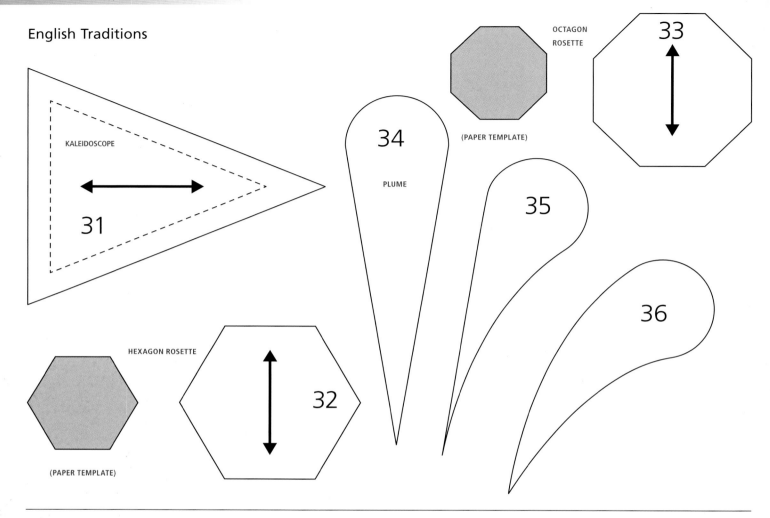

KALEIDOSCOPE

31

OCTAGON
ROSETTE

(PAPER TEMPLATE)

33

PLUME

34

35

36

HEXAGON ROSETTE

(PAPER TEMPLATE)

32

Taupe Tranquillity

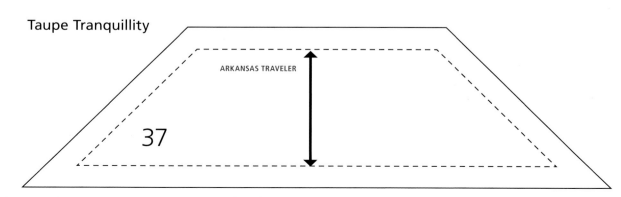

ARKANSAS TRAVELER

37

Japanese Odyssey

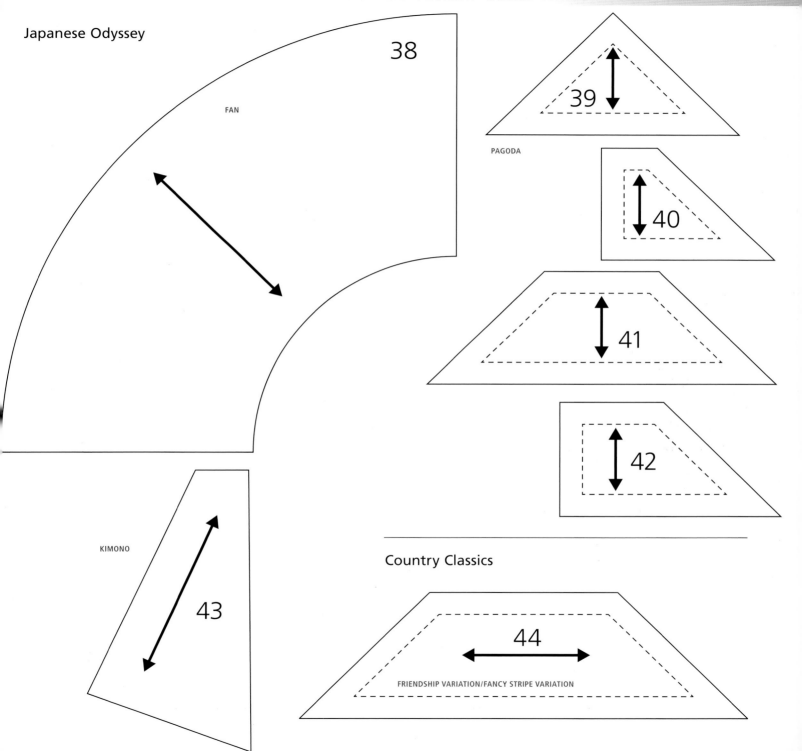

FAN

38

PAGODA

39

40

41

42

KIMONO

43

Country Classics

44

FRIENDSHIP VARIATION/FANCY STRIPE VARIATION

Index

Resources and credits

Clotilde
PO Box 7500
Big Sandy, TX 75755-7500
Tel: +00-1-800-545-4002
Email: customer_service@clotilde.com
www.clotilde.com
Fabrics and quilting supplies

eQuilter.com
5455 Spine Road
Suite E
Boulder, CO 80301
Tel: +00-1-303-527-0856
Email: service@equilter.com
www.eQuilter.com
Fabrics and quilting supplies

Hancocks of Paducah
3841 Hinkleville Rd
Paducah, KY 42001
Tel: +00-1-270-443-4410
Email: customerservice@hancocks-paducah.com
www.hancocks-paducah.com
Fabrics and quilting supplies

Homestead Hearth
105 Coal Street
Mexico, MO 65265
Tel: +00-1-573-581-1966
Email: info@homesteadhearth.com
www.homesteadhearth.com
Fabrics and quilting supplies

Keepsake Quilting
PO Box 1618
Centre Harbor, NH 03226
Tel: +00-1-800-525-8086
Email: customerservice@keepsakequilting.com
www.keepsakequilting.com
Fabrics and quilting supplies

Purl Soho
147 Sullivan Street
New York, NY 10012
Tel: +00-1-212-420-8798
www.purlsoho.com
Fabrics and quilting supplies

Shibori Dragon
1124 Gravelly Lake Drive SW
Lakewood, WA 98499
Tel: +00-1-253-582-7455
Email: shiboridragon@juno.com
www.shiboridragon.com
Japanese textiles and sashiko supplies

The City Quilter
133 West 25th Street
New York, NY 10001
Tel: +00-1-212-807-0390
Email: info@cityquilter.com
www.cityquilter.com
Fabrics and quilting supplies,
including Japanese

Contact the author through her website at
www.susanbriscoe.co.uk

Author's acknowledgments

I would like to thank my family and friends for their support; Guy, Fluff, and Takenoko; the quilt shops listed in the suppliers' section for all their assistance sourcing fabrics; Clover for their handy gadgets, Bernina—my 153 Quilter's Edition sewing machine that stitched everything beautifully; and finally, many thanks to all the team at Quarto for producing another beautiful book.

Credits